Start A
CAKE
BUSINESS
From Home

Alison C McNicol

How To Make Money
from your Handmade
Celebration Cakes,
Cupcakes, Cookies,
Cake Pops and more!

A Kyle Craig Publication

www.kyle-craig.com

First published in 2012 by Kyle Craig Publishing

Text and illustration copyright © Alison C McNicol

Design and illustration: Julie Anson @ The Great Little Design Co.

ISBN 978-1-908707-07-9

Contents

Introduction

The fact that you're reading this book means that you've probably already been thinking about turning your cake making and decorating talents into a business for a while.

Perhaps you've been making beautiful cakes for friends and family for quite some time, and been told on more than one occasion, "You should sell these/start a cake business/do this full time."

The question is—are you ready to turn this talent of yours into a "proper business"?

Maybe you're stuck in a 9 to 5 job that no longer challenges you, and just being able to make the same money doing what you love, from home, would be a dream come true.

Or you may be a stay at home parent, desperate to do something for "you" (and earn some much needed extra income while you're at it).

Or you may even have a much more commercial vision and dream of creating a brand—seeing your cakes and bakes on the pages of magazines, on the shelves of major stores and being eaten at high-profile celebrity parties!

Whatever you are dreaming of - anything is possible. With passion, skill, hard work and determination YOU CAN create your dream cake business.

Read on to find out how!

Good Luck! Alison x

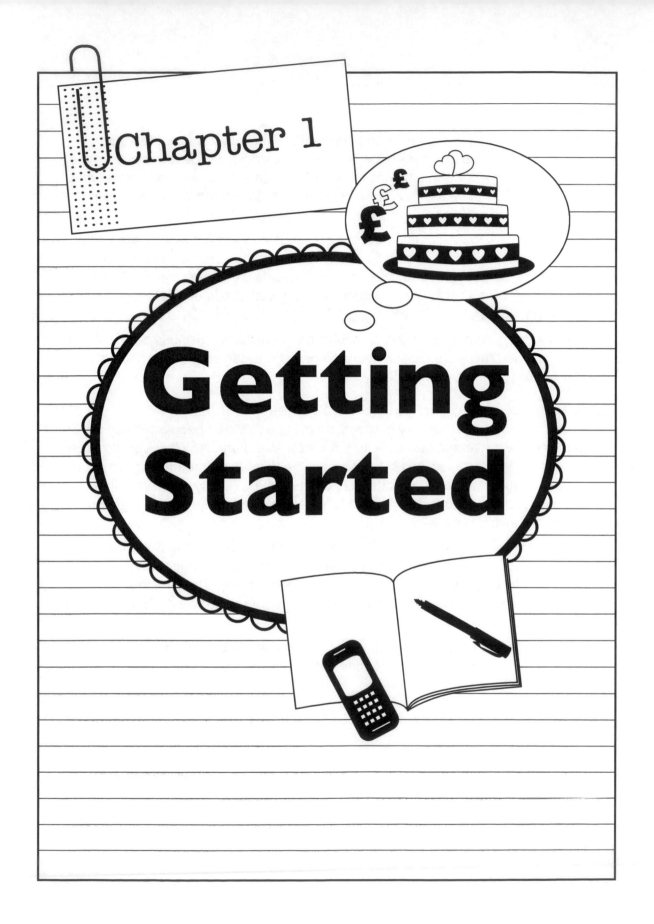

Chapter 1

Getting Started

Sweet Dreams!

Every single person will have a completely different picture of how they would like their dream cake business to be. And each business will be as unique as the person who owns it. So much depends on you as an individual—your personality, your skills, circumstances, environment, support network, family and financial situation and much more.

You will already know, from the reactions of friends and family to your cakes, that there can be a huge amount of satisfaction to be had from creating something that brings such pleasure to others. The personal rewards can be enormous. There's nothing better than seeing people smile, all as a result of something that you have created with your own fair hands!

But the reality of turning a rewarding hobby into a profitable business can be full of challenges, and there are a great many things to consider, so it's important to look at these closely before you proceed.

Are you cut out to run your own business?

Do you have the skills, not only to create amazing cakes that people will pay for, but to organise, promote and sell these in a business-like manner? What sacrifices are you willing to make to succeed? Do you have the drive and determination to put in the hours required to get a new business off the ground? What about your financial situation, support network, and personal life? Are you in the right place, right now, to start your own business?

And what about if/when your business becomes a huge success and you have more orders than you can cope with? Are you willing to work even longer hours? Take on staff? Move to a premises? Or will you decide, right from the start, that you only ever want this to remain a small, home-based part-time endeavour? Because that's fine too!

It's so important to consider all these aspects, right at the beginning. This will help you set goals, and boundaries, and formulate a business plan that is exactly right for YOU!

Now—there's just a few things to figure out before you get started. Are you ready?

What's Your Motivation?

It's good to have a very honest talk with yourself, at this early stage, to figure out what makes you tick. Try the checklist below, and circle what speaks to you. It's interesting to refer back to this as your business progresses.

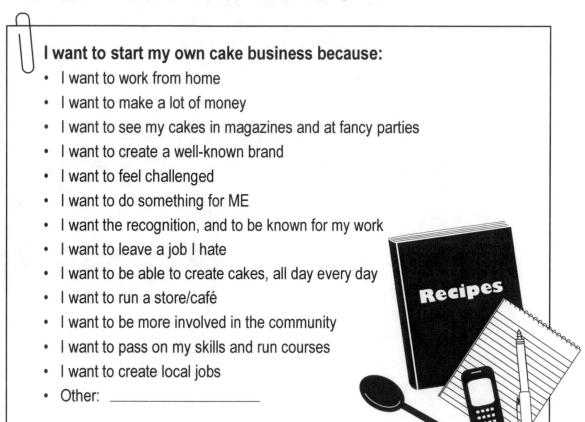

I want to start my own cake business because:

- I want to work from home
- I want to make a lot of money
- I want to see my cakes in magazines and at fancy parties
- I want to create a well-known brand
- I want to feel challenged
- I want to do something for ME
- I want the recognition, and to be known for my work
- I want to leave a job I hate
- I want to be able to create cakes, all day every day
- I want to run a store/café
- I want to be more involved in the community
- I want to pass on my skills and run courses
- I want to create local jobs
- Other: _____

Time For Some...Visualization

Starting your own cake business isn't *just* about making and decorating cakes and selling them to people! The whole point about working for yourself and launching a business is to create the most important thing in the world—your ideal life! Or working life at least! When you dream of starting your own business, no doubt you will be imagining the cakes you'll create and the people who will buy them... but without a doubt you will be imagining the LIFE you'll be leading as you do this!

The best thing about being your own boss it that *you* get to decide how *your* working life will be. Perhaps just the idea of being able to work from home making cakes every day is your idea of bliss. Or travelling all over the place to farmers markets and fairs, and meeting lots of interesting new people, and customers, floats your boat. The great thing is, *you* can decide what shape your life will take, and *you* have the power to make it all happen.

Take 5 minutes now to close your eyes and daydream about your new cake business life...how it feels, how it looks, where you are, what you are doing, and how things develop as your business grows.

Hold that picture in your mind...now it's time to start making your dreams a reality!

Imagine your ideal working day
- What time will you start work at?
- Where will you work from?
- Who will be there?
- What will the day hold?
- How many hours will you work?
- How will this fit in with family life?
- What will you make?
- What other tasks will you do?
- How will you feel?

Now imagine how this can be improved upon as you work hard to grow your business. What will the picture look like in 2 years...in 5 years?

What Are Your Expectations?

As well as imagining the look, feel and future of your potential new business, setting some clear goals right at the start helps keep you focused, and is a great way of motivating you and keeping you on track. Like anything in life, you'll get back what you put in—so if you're aiming high, then you need to be prepared to put in the hard work in order to reap the rewards.

Ask any creative business-person and they will tell you that, in order to make enough income to live on, or to replace a regular job, you'll need to work harder than you ever have in your life. Are you willing to give up your evenings and weekends at first, and see less of your friends and family? Does the idea of eating, sleeping and breathing your business appeal to you? Are you willing to do whatever it takes to make your business a success? If the answer to any of these is no, then that's absolutely OK. Not everyone is aiming for world domination, or to be the next Duff Goldman or Martha Stewart! You have to figure out what is right for *YOU*!

Are you willing to leave your comfort zone?

Perhaps you're not a natural salesperson? If you're incredibly shy, chances are that the idea of blowing your own trumpet, selling directly to the public at markets or fairs, managing a cake consultation meeting with a bride and groom, or being interviewed by your local paper brings you out in a cold sweat. Are you willing to take a deep breath and overcome your fears?

Or perhaps you don't consider yourself a natural "business" person. Many creative people are terrified at the idea of dealing with the paperwork involved in running a business. The thought of keeping accounts, filing tax returns and dealing with bureaucracy can be scary—but it's actually much simpler than you may think and that's what accountants are for!

Before you get started, have a serious think about what you ARE willing to do to achieve your business goals, what sacrifices you are willing to make, and what aspects of your life are simply non-negotiable. Doing so at this early stage is really helpful as once a new business begins, it can take over your life without you even realising it! Do you think you have what it takes to succeed?

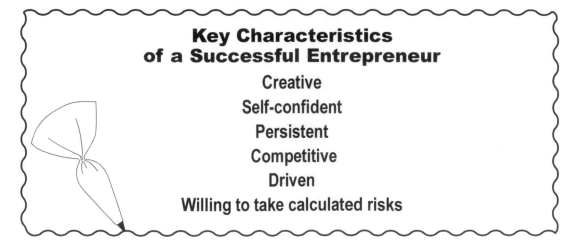

**Key Characteristics
of a Successful Entrepreneur**

Creative

Self-confident

Persistent

Competitive

Driven

Willing to take calculated risks

> "Making cakes as a business certainly changed things for me—I don't now sit at home doing a cake for the fun of it anymore. But it's an extremely happy and pleasurable business to run because people are generally buying cakes for celebrations."
> **Jane Asher**

Consider Your Ideal Working Life:

- How many hours per day/week am I willing to work?
- Am I OK with working weekends, and am I willing to give up my social life at first?
- How much cash do I have to get started, and can I survive financially while the business grows?
- What are my monetary goals?
- Do I want this to be a full-time occupation?
- How many cakes can I imagine making each week?
- Will I enjoy dealing with the public?
- Could I handle difficult customers and/or criticism or complaints?
- Can I handle the paperwork and official stuff involved in running a proper business?
- Am I willing to take on premises if necessary, or do I only want to work from home?
- Am I willing to employ others in order to grow the business?
- What scares me about this?

Find some...Inspiration

Whether it's creating a new cake design or imagining the possibilities for a new business, we all need plenty of inspiration to really get those creative juices flowing. There's nothing like checking out the competition, or seeking out other cake decorators or cupcake shop owners whose careers you admire (and perhaps envy!) to really give you a clear picture of the possibilities that are in store.

Who is your inspiration? Look around—what cake designers or shops do you admire? Check out their websites, look on food blogs, check out other cake business pages on Facebook and look at their pictures. What are they doing that you love? What would you do differently for *your* business?

For cake decorators, there has never been more opportunity to network and communicate with others. There are tons of amazing blogs, e-zines, magazines and websites out there bringing together fans of cake decorating from all over the world. Warning—it' easy to lose hours, days of your life online in the name of "research"!

STOP the...Procrastination

I don't know about you, but I can quite happily while away hours, days, weeks, even months daydreaming. In fact, I'm so full of wonderful ideas, I reckon I could quite easily make a full time career out of visualising and imagining all the wonderful things I could/would do…if only I had the time/tools/money/support etc!

Sometimes the idea of something can be so overwhelming, the task seems so massive, that we find ourselves putting off getting started day after day.

It can often seem easier to find a million reasons why you can't or shouldn't get started on an idea right away, but eventually, the desire to create wins through. And it's true what they say about baby steps/bite-sized chunks/one step at a time and all that. By breaking the task down into small achievable goals, and taking a deep breath and doing just one thing—suddenly you find yourself one step closer to your goal.

If you're still waiting for the "right" time to start your own business—it may never come. Will you ever have enough time/money/freedom/support/space/energy to fulfil your dreams? Maybe. Maybe not. Maybe you already have all of those things, but you just don't realize it. These days you really don't need thousands to start a small business. And even a few hours a week is enough to get going.

So—*what's stopping you*?

Prepare your...Situation

If you're currently working full-time, or your days are jam packed with childcare and family commitments it can be hard to find the time, let alone the energy, to get started on a new business.

If you're going to find the time to really commit to your new business, you need to treat your "cake business time" as an appointment that is just as important as any other. Just as you would a dentist appointment, or a meeting at your child's school, pencil your "*CBT*" into your diary, even if it's just a 2-3 hour shift once a week to begin with. Some shifts could be used to deal with the paperwork and "business" side of things, others could be spent creating new designs and photographing them for your portfolio.

In this book we'll look at what needs to be done, and in what order, so that you can break each task down into achievable chunks so that it won't become too overwhelming!

By making a conscious effort to schedule the time for your new venture, with each day that passes the task will feel less daunting—the more you do the more you will be inclined to do—and you'll be up and running before you know it!

Start With A Bang!
If at all possible, could you take a week's "cake holiday" from your job? I'm sure you'd much rather spend a week off work relaxing on a beach somewhere tropical, but dedicating a chunk of time could be just the boost you need to get started!

Assess Your Skills

It's one thing to be told by friends and family how wonderful your cake creations are, but it's quite another to deliver a product at a standard that people will pay good money for.

With cake decorating seeing a huge surge in popularity, many of us know a hobbyist cake decorator willing to make cakes for friends and relatives for love, or very little money…so for people to place an order and pay money for you to supply a celebration cake, yours need to be extra special and really stand out from the crowd.

If you've been decorating cakes for years as a hobby then clearly you will already have considerable skills—but do you have the level of expertise needed to meet the expectations of your potential customers?

Identify any areas where you feel you could benefit from extra practice or training—the greater the range of skills you have the more you will have to offer your customers!

Keep an eye on trends—cupcakes may still be going strong now, but in 2 years from now, those who focused purely on these may find themselves struggling as tastes evolve and the fad passes.

Keep an eye on the competition, but keep developing your own ideas and make sure your products have a unique edge to them—that way you will stay one step ahead of the crowd.

It's all about...Communication

Talk to friends and family, tell them your plans. When you've spent months excitedly planning your new business, it can sometimes be quite daunting to share your hopes and dreams with others. What if they laugh? What if they react negatively and tell you you're crazy? What if they just don't get it?

Well that's ok. Each of us operate differently, and for some people out there, the idea of giving up a well-paid career, or risking time and money on a "pipe-dream cake business" may seem absolutely crazy.

I've got this great idea! You know how I love baking...

There will always be people who won't quite understand what you're doing, and those who support you and can be relied upon to help out when the going gets tough.

Even the most negative feedback can be helpful—friends can troubleshoot and ask questions about your business plans that will highlight an area that perhaps you hadn't considered, and provide an objective eye.

Knowing that your friends and loved ones will be following your progress and asking how things are going on a regular basis can be a great motivator!

And by putting your plans "out there", it can set off a whole chain of events...one friend may mention you to a colleague and before you know it, you have your next big cake order!

What's Your Plan?

So—are you clear on what you want to achieve now? What are your goals?
How will your new cake business life look?

My Aims...	In 6 months	In 2 years	In 5 years
Working hours per week			
Working from this location			
Offer the following products			
Be selling this many cakes per week			
Have this many staff			
Premises?			
Pay myself this per month			
Other			
Other			

When I started my business, I was 23,
I had no business license, no tax ID. I didn't
know what I was doing! I started from home, and
was doing maybe a cake or two a month, here and there,
just to get the word out that there was somebody in
Baltimore making these kinds of cakes. It didn't become
my full-time money-maker, what paid my bills, for
a couple of years. The official opening of
Charm City Cakes was March 3rd of 2002,
which was the day I quit my full-time job!

**Duff Goldman,
Charm City Cakes/Ace of Cakes**

Go for it

No two days will be the same.

You'll find out your true strengths.

And your weaknesses.

You will learn more about yourself in that first year of business, than in all the previous years of working put together.

You'll surprise yourself, and be proud of yourself, on a daily basis.

If you don't give it a try, you'll never know!

Chapter 2

Working From Home

Home-Based Kitchens—State Regulations

Before you begin formulating a business plan based on baking from home, it's important to check the laws for your particular state and county to see if you are permitted to run a home-based food business.

There are certain rules and regulations that govern the food industry, and these are set by the individual states. There are currently 31 states that allow residents to bake from home for profit in some form, and other states that have major restrictions. These are called the Cottage Food Laws. You must check with your particular state in order to get complete details on how, what and where you may make and sell your products. Please refer to the Resources section at the rear of the book for contact details for your local state regulatory offices.

Not all state or local laws are the same, and it is the responsibility of the individual food processor to learn what laws and regulations are applicable to their residence. Food processors are allowed to sell their products at Farmer's Markets, to the general public and in some cases wholesale depending on the regulatory agency rules for sales and distribution.

What are *Cottage Food Laws*?

The term "*cottage*" originally referred to the family cottage (home) familiar to most rural communities. When we refer to the "*Cottage Food Law*" we are addressing legal tools employed by a state government to establish a legal arrangement for low risk food production prepared at a home residence.

A "*Cottage Food Production Operation*" involves a person using their own kitchen facility to produce food items that are not potentially hazardous, including bakery products, jams, jellies, candy, dry mixes, spices and some sauces.

"*Cottage Food Laws*" are different for every state so home-based bakers and food processors should check with their individual state regulatory agency to learn about specific rules, regulations and labeling requirements. It should be noted that there are states that have no "*Cottage Food Law*" at all and simply do not allow home food processors to produce food products from home. In these cases a licensed commercial kitchen must be used.

A "*Cottage Food Production Operation*" may or may not be exempt from inspection and licensing. In some states a compliance officer from the Department of Agriculture and Consumer Services will come to the food processor's home and inspect it. In addition, many food products, including those produced and packaged by a "*Cottage Food Production Operation*", may be subject to food sampling conducted by the regulatory agency involved to determine if a food product is misbranded or contaminated. Again, this will vary from state to state so you need to check locally.

It should also be mentioned that, not all areas of a state allow home food processing. There is a gray area involving individual cities, counties and towns with regard to "*Cottage Food Laws*" which may disallow home-based baking and food processing, thereby requiring the food processors to only prepare food from a licensed commercial kitchen.

States with *Cottage Food Laws*

The following states have *Cottage Food Laws* that allow home food processing:

- Arizona
- Florida
- Indiana
- Maine
- Michigan
- Missouri
- New Mexico
- Ohio
- Pennsylvania
- Texas
- Vermont
- Washington
- Wisconsin
- Arkansas
- Illinois
- Iowa
- Massachusetts
- Mississippi
- New Hampshire
- North Carolina
- Oregon
- South Dakota
- Utah
- Virginia
- West Virginia
- Wyoming

States with Restricted *Cottage Food Laws*

The following states currently have *Cottage Food Laws*, however the laws have some major restrictions:

- Alabama
- New Jersey
- Tennessee
- Kentucky
- New York

States with Pending *Cottage Food Laws*

The following states currently have Cottage Food initiative or legislation pending:

- California
- Georgia
- Maryland
- Nevada
- Colorado
- Louisiana
- Minnesota
- South Carolina

States with No *Cottage Food Laws*

The following states do not have cottage food laws:

- Alaska
- Delaware
- Idaho
- Montana
- North Dakota
- Rhode Island
- Connecticut
- Hawaii
- Kansas
- Nebraska
- Oklahoma

Leasing a Commercial Kitchen Space

If local laws prohibit you from running a home based food business, don't despair, there are still options available to you. Why not find a local incubator or commercial kitchen to rent. This allows you to do all your baking and cake making away from the home, but run all the other aspects of your business—admin, customer liason, marketing and pr etc. from home. This can also be a great alternative if space is tight, or you lack the funds to modify or adapt your home kitchen in order to satisfy the certification officer.

For more information on finding a kitchen space outside the home, see **Chapter 10**.

Home Is Where The Heart Is

One of the great things about working for yourself is the ability to create a working routine that suits you and your lifestyle. No more long commutes, less pressure on childcare needs, and being able to work as and when it suits you from the comfort of your own kitchen can be a major attraction when deciding to start a cake business.

But it goes without saying that running a new business from the family home will require changes that will affect everyone involved. A spare room may need to become your office space, the playroom cupboards may need to be cleared to allow for storage, and access to the kitchen may have to be prohibited during busy cake-making times. So it's important to discuss the potential changes with everyone involved and look at how they will be affected too. Starting a new business can be challenging and exhausting, so it's key that you have great support behind you.

Financial Considerations

Another major positive about working from home is that your set-up costs can be more manageable, and there's no rent to pay! You may well already have much of the equipment you need in place, but there will still be much to consider—and buy— to get yourself up and running. But there will still be some minor changes to your home set-up to be made before you're ready to launch, so let's look at what you'll need for a smooth home-working set-up.

Your mortgage company

If you intend to run a business from home, it is highly likely that, within the terms of your agreement, you are legally required to inform your mortgage provider or landlord. You should also check the title deeds of your property or your tenancy agreement as there may be a clause restricting or prohibiting you from doing so.

You may also be able to claim a proportion of your household costs as business expenses. This will depend on the number of rooms, and space used etc. You accountant will be able to advise how much you can claim for in relation to your household bills.

Dedicated Office area

Set up your office area somewhere in the home away from possible distractions— you really don't want to be dealing with a customer or speaking to a retailer about your products to the sound of the kids squabbling or cartoons in the background! Even if it's a nook under the stairs, a spare room or corner of the dining room, it's great to have an area that is all about business that you can close the door on and walk away from at the end of the day.

Dedicated Phone Line

It's never a good idea to use your home phone as a business line—just think of all the customer calls you could be missing while stuck on the phone for hours hearing all about your sister's latest work problems! You should definitely arrange a dedicated phone line just for your business calls. If possible, splash out on a cordless phone for the business line—at least that way you can keep it near you at all times, and dash to the "office" for privacy should a call come in while you're making the kids lunch! Make sure also that you have an answer-phone for calls during out of office hours. If you don't fancy installing an extra land-line, a dedicated mobile phone would also work well and a cheap contract or pay-as-you-go option can be a great way to get things up and running.

Computer and Super-fast broadband connection

As a business owner, you will almost certainly be spending lots of time online—whether it's researching suppliers and marketing/pr opportunities or updating and managing your Facebook business page or website—so if you haven't done so already, now is the time to upgrade your internet connection to the speediest available in your area. Because life really is too short to wait 3 minutes for a web page to load!

If your home PC is more than a few years old, it may be time to upgrade so that you have the latest software to create and handle your business needs, like Word documents for press releases, Adobe Acrobat for pdf's etc.

Digital Camera

Unless you're lucky enough to have a friend or partner who is a photography whizz, chances are you'll be taking lots of photos yourself for use on your website, online store, Facebook page. Invest in a good digital camera—it will pay for itself ten times over if it means you can do all your own product photography!

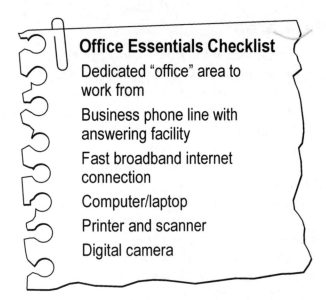

Office Essentials Checklist

Dedicated "office" area to work from

Business phone line with answering facility

Fast broadband internet connection

Computer/laptop

Printer and scanner

Digital camera

Before you schedule a visit from your local inspector, let's consider the areas they will be looking at:

- Your premises are thoroughly clean and in good repair
- Your premises have suitable and hygienic facilities for the preparation of food
- Your work area has walls and surfaces that are easy to clean and sanitise
- Your working procedures do not expose food to the risk of contamination
- Your ingredients are not stored in a way that allows the risk of cross-contamination
- Your refrigerator is operating at the correct temperature and offers no risk of cross-contamination
- You can present evidence of a regular cleaning schedule
- You have adequate facilities to wash and prepare food and cooking equipment
- You have a good supply of clean drinking water and drainage
- Have sufficient lighting and ventilation
- Have hygienic waste disposal
- Have implemented measures to protect against vermin

Basic Food Hygiene Considerations

Cleaning

It sounds simple enough, but many of us are guilty of forgetting—one of the most important things you can do is to make sure that your hands are clean at all times. This doesn't mean just passing your hands under the tap—give them a proper scrub with soap. In particular, remember to wash your hands:

After using the toilet
Before handling any food
After handling raw meat

If possible, remove any rings, watches and bracelets before you handle food. This is because bacteria can hide under these and get transferred to your food. Nail polish and nail art can also cause problems—so keep nails clean, short and natural.

Before you start preparing any food, make sure that the area you're working in and the utensils you're using are clean. Clean worktops thoroughly and wash utensils with washing up liquid and hot water, or use a dishwasher if you have one. Make sure you clean up any spilt food straight away. Change all tea towels, dishcloths and other cleaning materials regularly as these can harbor bacteria, especially if they are left damp.

Storing Food

Chances are you will be using your home refrigerator for both personal and business use, so it's important that **ALL** food that you prepare and store is handled correctly. Storing food in the wrong place or at the wrong temperature can lead to the growth of bacteria.

- Always check labels for guidance on where to store food.
- Make sure you keep your refrigerator at less than 5°C and your freezer at less than 18°C. This prevents bacteria from multiplying. You can use a thermometer to regularly check these temperatures.
- Store fresh and frozen food in the refrigerator or freezer as soon as possible after you have bought it. This is especially important if the weather is hot.
- Keep raw meat and seafood separate from other foods.
- Store raw meat in an airtight container at the bottom of the refrigerator to prevent juices or blood dripping onto other food.
- Defrost frozen foods in the refrigerator. Place them on a plate or in a container as they defrost so they don't drip onto or contaminate other foods.
- Don't store opened tins of food in the refrigerator—transfer the contents to a suitable airtight container instead.
- Allow food to cool to room temperature before you store in the refrigerator.

Preparing Food

There are a few points to remember when it comes to preparing your food.

- Don't handle food if you have stomach problems such as diarrhoea or vomiting, or if you're sneezing or coughing regularly.

- Check the food labels before you decide what to use. Shop-bought foods may come with two dates: a use-by date and a best before date. Don't use any foods that have passed their use-by date, even if you think they look fine, as they may not be safe to eat. However, you can use food after its best before date as this only refers to the quality of the food, rather than the safety of eating it. The only exception is eggs, which contain a type of bacteria called Salmonella that may multiply after the best before date. So always throw eggs away once this date has passed.

- Keep anything that should be refrigerated out of the refrigerator for as short a time as possible, especially if the temperature is high or the room is very warm.

- Always use different chopping boards and utensils to prepare raw meat or fish. This is because they contain harmful bacteria that can spread to anything they touch so they should be kept away from other foods. The bacteria are removed during cooking, but it's important not to let them come into contact with any food that you're not going to cook before eating it. You can buy colour-coded chopping boards (for example, red for raw meat and green for fruit and vegetables), which can help to prevent confusion.

Allergies

At some point you will find yourself dealing with a customer with some very specific requirements due to allergies of themselves or their guests.

One of the most common allergies, particularly in small children, can be peanut or nut allergies. In many cases, even the most tiny trace of nuts can cause a severe reaction—one reason why many food labels now contain information regarding whether the food item was prepared in an environment where there may be the possibility of exposure to nuts. With this in mind, in addition to obviously paying very close attention to all the ingredients you use for the actual cake and decorations, consider whether you can make your home and kitchen a nut-free zone, in order to confidently declare your cakes safe and nut-free.

Storage

Unless you're lucky enough to have a second, professional kitchen installed in your garage or outbuilding (like Bree in '*Desperate Housewives*'!) then it's likely that you will be using your home kitchen for all your baking and decorating.

Allocate a cupboard, separate to your family foodstuffs, for all your baking and decorating ingredients. Dry goods like flour, sugar etc. should be stored in sealed containers, not just the paper bags they came in. Any foodstuffs should be stored "off the floor", whether in cupboards or on a shelf unit.

You will also no doubt have a growing collection of non-food equipment that is threatening to take over you kitchen. Not to mention when you start buying cake boxes, boards and stands in bulk! Perhaps you could have a designated cupboard—in the spare room or garage, to store these. The more organised and easy to access your cake-making equipment is, the smoother your business will run.

Customer Consultations

As your business grows, it's likely that you will begin to have regular consultations with customers. Your home will be your showroom— does it reflect well on the business? This will be the first impression a customer has of you, so it's important to make the right one!

Consider where will you hold your consultations, and when is the best time to do them? If a busy working couple can only visit on a weekend or evening to discuss their wedding cake, how will that work if you have small children at home?

Do you have a dedicated space you can set aside, away from the distractions of family life? Can this room be "dressed" to impress—like a mini showroom with photos of your cakes, and any certificates or press features on the walls?

Even if it's the dining room which you dress for each visit, it's essential that you have a bright, clean professional looking area to meet your customers, so have a think about what your options are.

Pros and Cons of Working from Home

Pros	Cons
No travelling time—goodbye long commute!	Lack of structure—you need to be very self-disciplined to make the most of each working day
Low outgoings—no rent for premises	Food Safety and local/state compliance and some changes to home set-up required
Fits well with childcare	Balancing act—family needs and business can sometimes clash. Set boundaries, even though you are physically at home, advise when you are "working and not available"
Flexible work hours—you can work as and when time suits	Customer visits can disrupt family time
Proportion of home costs can be treated as a business expense	Loneliness—working alone can be a real shock if used to working in a team
Extra hands—family members can pitch in during busy periods	Cabin fever—working and living in the same place can become stifling. Make sure to get out and about marketing your business and networking.

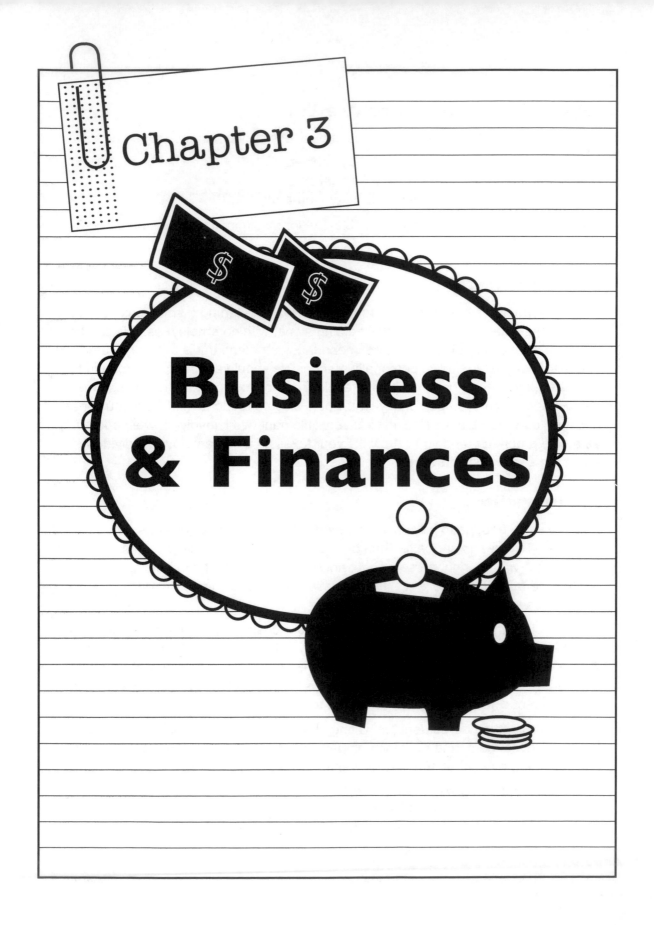

Chapter 3

Business & Finances

What Kind Of Business Are You?

At this stage, there are 3 obvious types of business structures to choose from *:

Sole Proprietor
Partnership
Limited Liability Company (LLC)

*there are various other options available, but for most small start-ups on of the 3 above should suffice.

Sole Proprietor

A Sole Proprietor is perhaps the most common way of starting a small business for many people starting out. If you are working alone, with no employees, this can be the simplest way to get started. It will mean that your company is unincorporated, and also that you are 100% personally responsible should anything go wrong in the business. If someone became ill as a result of one of your cakes, then a customer could in theory sue you personally. You would also be responsible for any business debts or loans. On the flip side, there's very little paperwork involved when operating as a sole proprietor, and you simply file your taxes as a self-employed individual, much the same as if you were a freelancer.

Partnership

If you're lucky enough to have a like-minded friend to start your business with, fantastic ! Two heads are better than one, and it can definitely be tons of fun sharing the journey with the right person. Right now, probably the last thing on your mind is "what if we fall out/wish to leave the business/sell our share" etc. But a little planning now can save a big headache in the long run.

What if your partner has a new baby, just as your business is taking off—have you agreed how much time off she will take? Or if you're willing to spend 12 hours a day, 7 days a week getting things going, but feel their contribution falls way short of that. Different work ethics and expectations can be the downfall of even the best friendships once business and money are in the mix.

You should draft an agreement , in writing, that outlines who is responsible for what, the initial investment and % of the company owned by each partner, and what will happen in the event that one partner wants to leave the business.

Be aware though that with a partnership, not only can you be held personally responsible for company debts in the same way as being a Sole Proprietor, but you are also liable for any and all business debts, even those run up by your partner.

This "joint and several liability" means you are each responsible both jointly, and individually in the event of the other person being unable to pay. So if your best friend is tons of fun and a great creative asset, but a bit free and easy with the cash, perhaps build into the agreement that any purchases over a certain amount must be agreed by both parties.

Limited Liability Company (LLC)

If you're keen to protect your personal assets from any business dealings, then an LLC could be for you. Many small business owners operate as an LLC as it allows them to keep their business and personal finances completely separate, and offers them personal protection should anything go wrong in business. There is of course more paperwork involved than with a Partnership or as a Sole Proprietor, but it could be worth it in the long run for peace of mind. An LLC can be owned by an individual or a group of people, so this could also offer a good alternative to a partnership (though still draw up a partnership agreement too).

Note—If you do become a Limited Liability Company, you should always use (LLC) at the end of your company name on all official paperwork, letterheads and on your website at the bottom. You don't, however, need to work it into your logo thankfully! We will look at the records you will need to keep in order to file your tax return later in this chapter.

Permits and Licenses

Regardless of whether you're planning on selling your cakes online, to local customers, at a few farmers markets, or targeting the big stores, if you're selling goods for a profit, then you are considered "in business". As well as the Food Hygiene permits we discussed in the last chapter, anyone in business needs to have the right license, permits and follow the tax laws for their state or county. Here are a few essentials:

Get A Business License
This is an annual license, usually purchased via your county clerk, that allows you to operate a business within your state.

DBA (Doing Business As)—Ficticious Business Name
Assuming you've given your business it's own name, then you will be "Doing Business" under that name, not your own name, so you need to file a Ficticious Business Name, also called a DBA through your county clerk.

Business Bank Account

Not only can it be illegal to run your business through your personal bank account, having a separate account for your business will make things way easier when it comes to keeping your personal and business finances separate and for preparing tax returns and filing accounts. You can open the account in the name of your business once you have filed your DBA.

When opening a new account—check the small print for charges. If you think you will be regularly depositing cash and cheques (say, after county fairs and farmers markets), choose a bank with a local branch, and also check the fees for each deposit. I always open a second business account for tax money which I put away on a regular basis—this keeps your tax money safe and separate from the day-to-day business funds—a real bonus when it's time to pay tax, you can sleep at night knowing that it is safely tucked away !

Federal Tax ID

Also known as an **EIN** (*Employer Identification Number*), this is a number the IRS supplies to most business entities. If your business operates as a partnership, corporation or has any employees then you need to apply for one of these. If you are a Sole Proprietor, then you do not require one—your Social Security number is all that is needed when filing taxes.

Insurance

There are various types of Insurance to consider:

Health Insurance: You may already be covered by your partner's employee-sponsored health plan, but if not it's important to know that you have sufficient cover in the event of illness.

Income Replacement Insurance: What would happen if you were ill and unable to work or run the business? Aimed at self-employed individuals, for a monthly fee—based on the amount of cover and what your usual/desired monthly income amount is—you can insure against being unable to operate due to illness. In the event that you have a serious illness, the insurance would pay out an agreed amount of money per month for a set amount of time.

Public Liability Insurance: This covers you in the event that someone sues you as a result of any illness or injury caused by your product. Given the potential risks for a food business, this would be considered essential.

Trademarks and Intellectual Property

So you have decided on your company name, and you're ready to start getting your website and marketing materials ready. While it may seem rather early to start thinking about having such a successful product that others may want to imitate, it's very important to protect yourself right from the beginning. Check out Chapter 5 for more information on choosing the right name for your business.

What is a trademark?

- A trademark provides legal protection in the marketplace for the name of your product or business name and is defined as any word, name, symbol or device used to distinguish one producer's goods from others.

- A trademark is a key piece of intellectual property (IP) that is vital to the future success of your product or brand.

- You need to protect your product's name right at the beginning, before you start selling it or introducing it to the marketplace. If you don't, you could risk someone else coming along and registering it and contesting your rights to use that name.

- You also need to register it right at the beginning to be absolutely sure that you are not infringing on someone else's registered trademark.

- It can take up to a year to have your trademark formally approved by the USPTO, so during that time you should use the TM symbol next to your product's name, to let the public know that you are claiming it as your mark.

Searching for and Registering a Trademark

To search for and/or register a trademark, go to the USPTO website (www.uspto.gov) and click on the Trademarks tab.
Under the Basics tab you will find "Where Do I Start".

Protect Yourself!

A google search for *"Trademark Registering"* will throw up hundreds of companies offering to file your TM application, often for a considerable fee. Obviously these companies have a level of expertise in dealing with what may at first be an overwhelming and confusing amount of information, but if you want to avoid unnecessary costs it really is worth trying to do this yourself, or asking a business-whizz friend to help!

Don't Freak Out!!

If the thought of all these forms and rules and regulations is bringing you out in a cold sweat—don't panic! I've tried to provide you with lots of information on the stuff you MIGHT need, and you certainly don't need to worry about ALL of these things right at the beginning...but when the time comes and our business grows, it's good to already have an idea of the kind of stuff that will need to be addressed. Growing a business is a gradual process, and if you plan ahead a little, and ask for help a lot, you'll have no problems dealing with each of these little challenges as you go along.

Creating A Business Plan

Now that all the set-up is done, you can really get this show on the road! Next up, you'll need to do a business plan. Sounds scary? Well chances are, you've actually already thought about most of the aspects involved and can easily answer many of the questions. And writing a proper business plan can also throw up some really interesting questions that you may not have yet considered.

Think of a business plan simply as a list of questions on a form or template. Deal with each question as it comes up, and see what your response is. Take your time to consider each carefully—you're planning the next few years of your working life after all, so there's no need to rush!

By having those questions and answers in front of you, it can not only help you map the way forward for your business and help you define your goals in real, concrete terms, but it can be an excellent reference tool as your business grows. It's so easy to get caught up in the day-to-day running of a business that we lose sight of our original aims, so once completed, you can refer to it often to see if you're on track.

Each chapter of this book will cover a different area from your business plan—so you can refer back to these pages once you've finished reading!

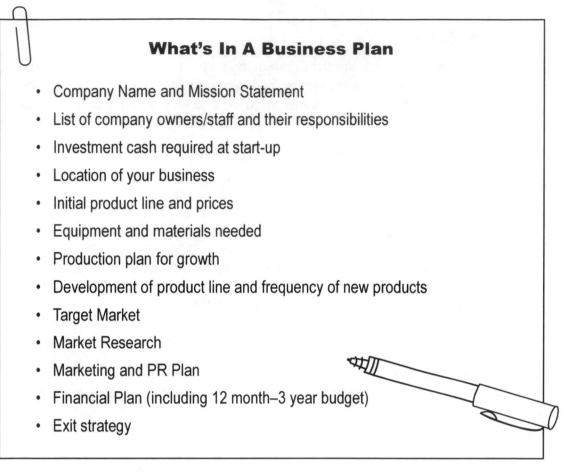

What's In A Business Plan

- Company Name and Mission Statement
- List of company owners/staff and their responsibilities
- Investment cash required at start-up
- Location of your business
- Initial product line and prices
- Equipment and materials needed
- Production plan for growth
- Development of product line and frequency of new products
- Target Market
- Market Research
- Marketing and PR Plan
- Financial Plan (including 12 month–3 year budget)
- Exit strategy

The great news is that there are tons of free resources out there and many Business Plan templates available.

Free Business Plan Templates

SCORE: Service Corps of Retired Executives
www.score.org/template_gallery.html

SBA: Small Business Administration
www.sba.gov/starting_business/planning/writingplan.html

WBDC: Women's Business Development Center
www. Wbdc.org.tools/develop/develop.asp

Getting Help

Starting your own business needn't mean going it alone—here's a huge amount of free help and advice available out there, so make the most of it and you'll soon be on the road to success, and meet some amazing and inspirational people along the way!

SCORE (Service Corps of Retired Executives)

SCORE is a nonprofit association dedicated to educating entrepreneurs and helping small businesses start, grow, and succeed across the US. SCORE is a resource partner with the U.S. Small Business Administration (SBA), and has been mentoring small business owners for more than forty years. With a network of over 13,000 volunteer mentors, across 364 local chapters, SCORE also offers local business workshops and tons of free online business tools. **www.score.org**

SBDC (Small Business Development Center)

This is a free program run by the Small Business Administration (**www.sba.gov**) and is available in every state in the US. Visit their website to find your local office.

Your Local College or University

Often a business student or graduate may be able to assist you draw up and review your business plan, or undertake market research—in exchange for extra college credit. It's definitely worth looking into this untapped resource, and you could find yourself with an excellent source of help for all manner of business needs! Students are always looking for extra cash, and could be that helping hand you need next time you have a large order to fulfil or trade show to attend!

Find A Mentor

Perhaps someone in your circle of friends or contacts already knows a successful entrepreneur who would be willing to meet up for a coffee and a chat. Or maybe you've met someone through a local fair or group who impressed you with what they've achieved with their business already. Practical advice from someone who has already been through what you're embarking on and has lived to tell the tale is worth its weight in gold.

Taking Payments

Years ago, the only way to take credit or debit card payments from customers involved getting a merchant account via your business bank, and paying to buy or rent a terminal—a fairly lengthy and costly process.

Nowadays, companies like Paypal have made the process much simpler. Anyone with a computer can now take credit or debit card payments—either over the phone, by emailing their customer an invoice and payment request, or via their website.

Depending on your turnover and business needs, paypal offer various levels of accounts: Virtual Terminal/Website Payments Standard/Website Payments Pro etc.

These accounts tend to charge a small monthly fee, then paypal take a percentage of each transaction value. So while it's not free, it could be the most cost-effective solution for your business.

www.paypal-business.co.uk/how-to-take-online-payments-with-paypal

SQUARE

Square is a fantastic new device that attaches to your smart phone and allows you to swipe and take payments from cards on-the-spot. This fantastic new gizmo was designed especially for the small business owner who needs to take card payments from customers from a variety of locations. For a fee of 2.75% of each transaction, square allows you to process card payments and the funds will reach your account the very next business day.

So if you need to take payments at events, markets or other areas away from your home, Square could be the perfect solution!

www.squaredup.com

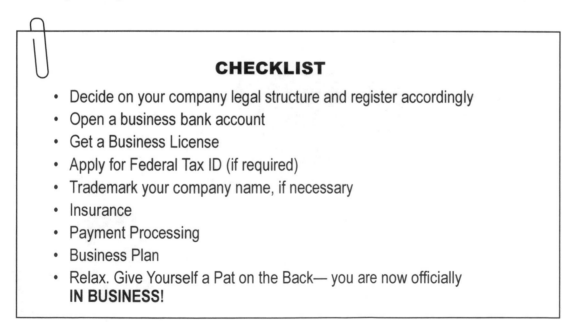

CHECKLIST

- Decide on your company legal structure and register accordingly
- Open a business bank account
- Get a Business License
- Apply for Federal Tax ID (if required)
- Trademark your company name, if necessary
- Insurance
- Payment Processing
- Business Plan
- Relax. Give Yourself a Pat on the Back— you are now officially **IN BUSINESS**!

Chapter 4

Pricing For Profit

How Much Should I Charge For My Cakes?

This is one of the most frequently asked questions by cake decorators when they begin to sell their cakes. Setting a price structure is one of the most difficult parts of any business. Finding the right price point requires research of your competitors' prices, and a solid understanding of your own costs. You don't want to sell yourself and your talents short, but neither do you want to shock your customers with high prices, and leave them feeling like they paid too much, or even worse—have a customer argue about the price of your cake. Let's look at some of the common questions about the pricing issue.

Am I charging too much for my cakes?
It's doubtful. The most common problem with cakes is **underpricing**.

I don't feel right charging very much—I'm just starting out.
It is natural, when you are starting your cake business, to feel unsure of your skills, and hesitant about charging very much for your cakes. The first thing to remember is that we are our own worst critics. When YOU value your cakes and price them appropriately, your customers will too.

I have read that a good way to price cakes is to charge for the cost of ingredients times 2 (or 3).
The "ingredients times 2 or 3" method of pricing is arbitrary and not rooted in any kind of business theory. In my general experience, this method results in **grossly underpricing** your product. The cost of the cake lies not in the ingredients, but in the time and skill invested.

How do I know what people will pay for a cake in my community?
Do some research and see what other cake makers are offering and charging in your area. Set your prices close to theirs, or maybe *slightly* lower if you are still building your skill level. Although tempting, do NOT massively undercut them—this is a disservice to them, and to other decorators in your community.

But I called the local cake store, and their prices are really high. I can do it so much cheaper than that!
The local cake store is charging what they need to charge in order to pay rent, utilities, wages, and keep a roof over the head of the owner. If you significantly undercut their prices, you are not only lowering the value of cake in your community, but you could affect their business enough that they have to lay off employees, or

even close. Even though you don't have the overheads of a cake storefront, you owe it to the cake decorating community to maintain the value of your goods. There is no honour or pride in being the "cheap cake lady". Also, you run the risk of antagonizing them if you undercut their prices significantly. You may one day want to build a relationship with that cake shop. Professional relationships can enhance your business reputation and increase your bottom line through referrals! Don't think: "Their prices are way too high." Think: "Wow! Look what a custom cake is worth!"

Publix sells their cakes for $15—I can't match that price, much less beat it!

Never, ever compare your prices to a grocery store! People can't get the same cake there that they get from you. That cake at Publix was probably made months ago, flash-frozen, and shipped to the store, where an employee working as quickly as he/she could frosted it with icing from a bucket, and maybe added some airbrushing or buttercream roses. That employee probably had 50 other cakes to complete in the same shift. The difference between your cake and grocery store cake can be likened to the difference between a couture dress and a shift from Walmart! Say you went to a seamstress, consulted with her about the perfect fabric and cut for your body type, discussed your coloring, took measurements, went back for several fittings, and in the end had an exquisite dress, hand-made with excruciating attention to detail, perfect for your body. When the seamstress required payment, you would not tell her that a Walmart dress cost $29.99, so that's all you should pay. There is just no comparison!

People around here are used to grocery store prices, they won't pay much more than that.

You'd be surprised. It won't take long for your customers to realize that you are providing the kind of cake that a supermarket simply can't. Will Publix match a baby shower cake to an invitation? Will they accept fabric swatches of bridesmaids' wedding dresses to ensure a perfectly color co-ordinated wedding cake? Will they respond to multiple emails from a mother who's worried about making her daughter's bridal shower perfect in every way? No!

Someone complained about the price and said I charge too much!

Then that person is probably not meant to be your customer. Do they complain about the price at the hairdresser? At the local store? Probably not. If they will complain to you about the price, imagine what else they will complain about. If you let them talk you down in price, you are setting a very bad business precedent.

I can't charge that much, it's just cake!

"Just cake" can be found in the freezer at CostCo for $12. If you are going to sell your cakes, it's important to eliminate the phrase "it's just cake" from your vocabulary. Custom cakes and cookies are edible works of art that require skill and artistry, and can take days to complete. Duff Goldman, the owner and star of the US bakery and TV show "Ace of Cakes", has a $1,000 minimum for a Charm City Cake! (Not that I'm suggesting you start *quite* that high!!)

If I charge too much, I might lose the order!

And? Do you need to make a sale where you end up making below minimum wage or even losing money?

Pricing Each Cake

There are various ways of working out your pricing, and therefore your profit margins. It all depends on how much you can make each cake for, how much you need to earn, and what you can charge in your area.

Some people may start with the resale price—what they feel they can charge in their area, minus the cost of making the cake, and what's left is their profit/hourly rate. Say the average price for a 14" round novelty cake in your area is around $45-55. The ingredients cost you $15 to make, leaving a gross profit of $30. If it took you an hour to bake the cake, and another hour to decorate it, that works out at $15/hour wages for you. Not including the time spent consulting with the customer and admin. Happy with that?

Decide on the absolute minimum that you're happy to work for. If a potential cake order looks like it's going to earn you less than your set minimum, which may be £10/hour, it may be time to raise your prices! The more intricate and time consuming a cake— clearly a 4-tier wedding cake will require much more time and skill than the average birthday cake—the more expensive it will of course be, mainly due to the additional labour costs. Another method is to have a set, or minimum mark-up on each cake.The ideal mark-up to aim for is 50-70%.

If you wish to make a 70% profit per order:

Cake costing $15 with 70% profit: ($15 ÷ 30 x 100) = $50 selling price.

To figure out how much each cake costs to make, there are four elements to consider:

1. Cost of Ingredients
To know how much to charge, you must understand how much you are spending. It takes a time investment to calculate your ingredient costs, but it is vital to understanding what a cake costs you to make. Don't forget the cost of the cake boxes and boards, foil, and dowels etc.

2. Cost of your Time (labor cost)
When you start thinking about it, the time you spend on a cake is so much more than just the time spent decorating. There is time spent consulting with the customer, planning a design, shopping, baking, cooling, making fillings, frostings, fondant, and sometimes custom work like fondant or gumpaste toppers or figurines. You deserve to be compensated a fair hourly rate for the time you spend on a cake. Don't forget cleanup time! We've all seen what our kitchens look like after a big cake!

3. Cost of Overheads
When you bake a cake, you use your oven, your utilities, your pans, your mixer, your dishwasher, and soap. These things all required an initial investment by you, and a nominal fee for their use should be added to the cost of the cake.

4. Delivery costs
Your customer's wedding venue is two hours away and she wants the cake delivered and set up? Then you must certainly be compensated for your time, your gas, and wear and tear on your vehicle. Remember to charge for the entire round-trip!

Watch The Pennies...
Only by factoring in every single costing, right down to the teaspoon of vanilla extract, can you be sure you know exactly how much you are personally spending to create each cake. Calculating your labor costs can be trickier, and something that you will get better with the more cakes you do.

Buy Wholesale!

Buying your ingredients, and packaging supplies, in bulk is pretty essential if you want to maximize your profits. Often space can be an issue, and while you may not be ready to commit to 1000 cupcake boxes, I'm sure that committing to even 250 from a wholesale packaging supplier will be give you a much cheaper cost per unit than buying 10 at a time from a standard retailer.

Check out the Resources at the rear of this book for some suggested wholesalers.

Finding Good Suppliers

Price

Price is king. Paying even a few pennies more on each item can have a real effect on your profit margins, so negotiate hard and shop around for the best price. It may be that one wholesaler is cheaper than others for flour and sugar, but you can get a better price on fondant from another. Do your research and price compare!

Quality

Often, there's no such thing as a bargain, and while one supplier may offer a cheaper price, is the item up to the quality standards you require. Quality vs price is a fine balancing act.

Availability & Reliability

The cheapest supplier in the world is no use to anyone if they cannot supply regular stocks of the items you most need. Discuss with them availability—how long does it take them to re-stock items once they sell out. If you rely on just one supplier for your fondant and they suddenly run out when you have tons of orders, you'll waste valuable time scrabbling round finding a new supplier. Don't put all your eggs in one basket, so to speak!

What to Charge Friends and Family

Yes, this can be a tough one. There are a lot of factors at play here. Things to consider: do you have time to do the cake? Do you WANT to do the cake? How close are you to the person requesting the cake? Do you owe them a favour? Will this kind of cake add to my portfolio, and therefore give me a chance to try a new area

of design? I can't tell you how much to charge friends and family, but here are some options to consider:

Have a standing arrangement for everyone
If you offer to do the cake, it is free. If they request the cake, they pay for it (either full price, discounted some percentage, or ingredients only).

Different standing arrangement
If the person requesting the cake lets you have free reign of the design, the cake is free (or charged ingredients-only). If the person is going to get picky about design and act like a customer, then he/she can pay like a customer. This is a great way to practice new techniques you've been dying to try,
and get some new cakes in your portfolio.

Blanket discount
Offer all friends and family a standard discount off your regular prices—15%, 25%, 50%, whatever you are comfortable with.

Whatever you decide, don't feel obligated to make a cake for every family function, or every family/friend who wants one. There are only so many hours in the day! It's ok to say you're too busy, especially if it's a last-minute request.

Cakes for PR or Charities

You may be approached by local charities, schools or organisations to donate a cake for their upcoming event, and it's importantly to choose wisely as clearly you won't be able to say YES to everyone! It's always lovely to be able to support a worthy cause, but it's also crucial to put your business head on and think about what you and your business can gain from the opportunity. Will the local paper be covering the event, and can you be guaranteed that your cake, and name of your company, can be mentioned/featured in the piece? In exchange for the cake can you set up a table showcasing your cakes and giving out flyers and cards? Do they have a large membership, a newsletter, or a lot of Facebook followers—if so, can they give you a mention/advert/news story that goes out to all these people, in exchange for your cakes?

Always think "how can doing this help me reach new customers?"

INGREDIENTS: Cost Per Ounce/ml			
Item	Size of full pack	Price $	Cost/oz/ml
Basics			
Flour (self raising)			
Flour (plain)			
Sugar (granulated)			
Sugar (caster)			
Sugar (brown)			
Sugar (muscovado)			
Eggs			
Butter			
Milk			
Baking Powder			
Bicarb Soda			
Vanilla Essence			
Fruit cakes			
Sultanas			
Currants			
Raisin			
Walnuts			
Almonds (ground)			
Almonds (chopped)			
Lemons			
Glace cherries			
Spices			
Ginger			
AllSpice			
Nutmeg			
Toppings			
Fondant			
Confectioners Sugar			
Royal Icing Mix			
Sundry			
Sundry			

BASIC VANILLA CAKE: COSTINGS

Ingredient	15cm/6"		8cm/7"		20cm/8"		25cm/10"		30cm/12"		35cm/14"	
	Amt	Cost	Amt	Cost	Amt	Cost	Amt	Cost	Amt	Cost	Amt	Cost
Flour (self raising)												
Flour (plain)												
Sugar (granulated)												
Sugar (caster)												
Eggs												
Butter												
Milk												
Baking Powder												
Bicarb Soda												
Vanilla Essence												
Sundry												
Sundry												
Greaseproof												
TOTAL $												

CAKE COVERINGS/FILLINGS: COSTINGS		15cm/6"		8cm/7"		20cm/8"		25cm/10"		30cm/12"		35cm/14"	
		Amt	Cost	Amt	Cost	Amt	Cost	Amt	Cost	Amt	Cost	Amt	Cost
Ingredient													
Marzipan													
Royal Icing													
Fondant/Sugarpaste													
Buttercream													
Jam													
Chocolate Ganache													
Flavorings													
Colorings													
Other													
Other													
Other													
Decorations													
Piped Buttercream													
Piped Royal Icing													
Sugarpaste													
Colorings													
Other													
Other													
Other													
TOTAL $													

TIERED WEDDING CAKE: TOTAL COSTINGS				
	Tier 1	Tier 2	Tier 3	Tier 4
	15cm/6"	20cm/8"	30cm/12"	35cm/14"
Cakes				
Fillings				
Coverings				
Decoration 1				
Decoration 2				
Decoration 3				
Decoration 4				
Dowels				
Cake Boards				
Box(es)				
Other				
Other				
Other				
Other				
Cake Total $				
Labor				
Delivery				

"How I Did It"

"I contacted a celebrity management agency and told them about what I do and offered to send samples of my cupcakes and cake pops. They then contacted me and asked me to do cupcakes for a party for a famous model. They were really happy with them so then I made cake pops for another high profile event too, which was exciting. As a result, my cakes were featured in OK magazine, along with a credit and mention of my website at the end. I did supply them free for PR, but you have to weigh up the costs, and it was relatively cheap to make the cakes, but it would have been really expensive to pay for the PR I received so it was definitely worth it!"

Kathryn Carter, The Kooky Cake Company

Cake Whizz!

I hope I have provided you with enough information in this chapter, and book, to allow you to cost out your cakes manually, and create your own invoices etc. using a regular computer. This is the way most cake makers have been doing things for years.

But I've felt for a long time that there could be a better way, an easier way, to do all the admin and paperwork that a cake business needed on a daily basis. While I was researching this book I spoke to hundreds of cake makers who felt the same way. Many were muddling through with little spreadsheets, excel sheets and invoicing systems that meant they weren't always entirely sure exactly how much they were spending or making on each cake order, and they were spending so much time and energy on the admin side of running their businesses, when they'd much rather be doing the fun cake-making part!

And so my quest began. I conducted tons of research, and spoke to hundreds of cake business owners about what their needs were. I worked closely with a great software developer, did dozens of trials with other cake business owners, and the result is, if I do say so myself, the rather fantastic '*Cake Whizz*'.

Cake Whizz is a clever little piece of software that does all the things a busy cake business owner needs. It calculates the price of every single cake you make, right down to the last teaspoon of vanilla essence. When the price of an ingredient changes, CLICK, you simply update it on your system and it updates the costings of every single recipe and pending cake order.

And speaking of orders, you simply input the details of a cake order, and click to calculate exactly how much it will cost you to make. You can factor in things like labor costs, local sales tax, discounts, % mark-up, and calculate the exact profit margins on each order, and then click and create quotes and customized invoices for your customers.

A customer database keeps track of every order, all overdue and pending payments, and monthly totals to date. You can view customer contact information, birthdays and anniversaries, and order history, and create anniversary alerts—which is great for contacting existing customers in advance of each occasion—a great way to get follow-up business!

Every new order is automatically added to the planning calendar, which you can add other things into yourself, and view by the day, week, month or year.

Cake Whizz will even create a shopping list, based on whatever upcoming orders you select, so you know exactly what ingredients are required to fulfill them—never be caught short and run out of anything again!

I'm absolutely delighted with *Cake Whizz*, and the feedback I've had from the hundreds of people who are already using it has been amazing.

But please don't take my word for it—visit the website and have a look for yourself! And if you decide that it's just what you need, there's a special promotional discount code, only for readers of this book, supplied at the end of the book.

www.cakewhizz.com

Chapter 5

Branding Your Business

my brand

A Brand New You!

No matter how big or small your aims are for this new business, it's important to have a clear image of how you see your "brand" right from the start. Nowadays, even small home-based businesses present themselves in highly professional, stylish and creative ways that could rival even the "big boys"! You only have to look online and Facebook to see thousands of talented home-based cake makers who have taken the time to create a unique visual identity for their small businesses—it really is the key to being taken seriously these days.

Now this doesn't mean that you have to spend thousands of pounds on expensive designers—whether you go for just a great logo and a smart website to begin with, or you're planning big things and decide to Trademark and protect your company name (more of this later), getting your "brand" right is the first step to having a successful business.

Fake it 'Till You Make It (or Bake it!)

You may currently be only making cakes for family and friends and just getting started selling to the public—but present yourself and your cake company in the right way and customers could quite easily assume that they're dealing with an already highly successful local cake company.

Now I'm certainly not suggesting that you start misleading people about the true nature of your business, for there is absolutely nothing wrong with being a cake maker building an exciting new company on your own, from home, and often that can be a key part of your appeal. The message is that it pays to be confident and act as though you're already a success, right from the start. You'll send out the right message, come across as truly professional, and gain the respect and attention you and your cake creations deserve!

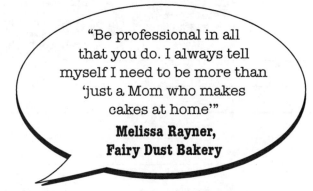

"Be professional in all that you do. I always tell myself I need to be more than 'just a Mom who makes cakes at home'"

**Melissa Rayner,
Fairy Dust Bakery**

Identify Yourself: The Key Elements of a Great Brand

Image/Personality

What do you want your company to be known for? Fun, novelty cakes? Sophisticated wedding cakes? Organic ingredients?

Choose a Name

Don't let it pigeon hole you i.e. *Claire's Cupcakes* or *Wanda's Wedding Cakes*. Think about not only what you are making now, but what you could potentially make in the future. Claire could find that the whole cupcake trend starts to fade and she'd like to do more birthday cakes, but people assume she only does cupcakes...and Wanda finds she's not being approached to do birthday cakes during the rest of the year when the wedding season is over...all because their names gave the public the wrong message right from the start!

Mission Statement

Can you describe, in no more than 100 words, the essence and unique qualities of your brand/company? For example: *"Claire's Crazy Cakes specializes in creating fun, kooky and unique celebration cakes for every occasion. Dare to be different."* Or: *"Belinda's Boston Bakes and Cakes creates delicious home-baked treats using all natural ingredients and traditional East Coast family recipes."*

See the different impressions each gives?

Have a look at the keywords below and circle those that you feel best describe your ethos, your products, or your ideal brand image:

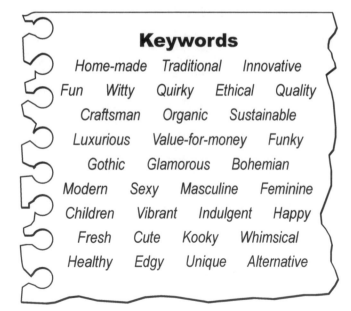

Keywords

Home-made   Traditional   Innovative

Fun   Witty   Quirky   Ethical   Quality

Craftsman   Organic   Sustainable

Luxurious   Value-for-money   Funky

Gothic   Glamorous   Bohemian

Modern   Sexy   Masculine   Feminine

Children   Vibrant   Indulgent   Happy

Fresh   Cute   Kooky   Whimsical

Healthy   Edgy   Unique   Alternative

Other words to describe your ethos/image:

Now…time to brainstorm some ideas for names, and decide on your mission statement.

Company Name Ideas:

Mission Statement:

Check your Company Name

Before you set your heart on a company name and start spending money on website domains and logos, it's important to double check that someone else isn't already out there trading under the same name.

First up, check in the kind of areas you'll be trading in initially. Look on Facebook and see if there are any other cake businesses with a similar name to yours. Do a Google search and see what comes up. If you're in luck so far, next step is to check with all the relevant official agencies to see if anyone in the US is trading under that name.

At state/local level you should look up the website of your state Corporation Division. Most will offer online searches where you simply type in to search for a business name. You can find a list and links to each state website at:
www.secstates.com

All clear at state level? Check that no big national companies are trading under your name or similar by checking at the US Patents and Trademarks Office:
www.uspto.gov

Once you have checked thoroughly and have the all clear, you are ready to register your company name and should file what is known as a DBA ('doing business as') registration with your county clerk.

If you have BIG plans for world domination, it's worth checking your potential business name in all the major English-speaking countries—USA, UK, Canada, Australia and New Zealand!

My company Name Is Going To Be:

So you have decided on your company name. While it may seem rather early to start thinking about having such a successful company that others may want to imitate, it's very important to protect yourself right from the beginning.

Now obviously if your aims are simply to create a successful part or full-time business from home, serving only your local area, then this section probably isn't really relevant to you. But in case any readers have HUGE plans for world cake-domination and want to create a massive US chain of cake stores or international brand, here's how to Trademark your company name!

Trademarking Your Company Name

What is a trademark?

- A trademark provides legal protection in the marketplace for the name of your product or business name and/or Logo, and is defined as any word, name, symbol or device used to distinguish one producer's goods from others.

- A trademark is a key piece of intellectual property (IP) that is vital to the future success of your product or brand.

- You need to protect your name right at the beginning, before you start selling it or introducing it to the marketplace. If you don't, you could risk someone else coming along and registering it and contesting your rights to use that name.

- You also need to register it right at the beginning to be absolutely sure that you are not compromising someone else's registered trademark.

- It can take up to a year to have your trademark formally approved, so during that time you should use the TM symbol next to your company name or logo to let the public know that you are claiming it as your mark.

Searching for and Registering a Trademark

You can search for and register trademarks at the USPTO (US Patents and Trademarks Office) at **www.uspto.gov**. Click on the Trademarks Tab. Under 'Basics', you will find 'Where Do I Start?'

Get a Domain Name

Your domain name, or URL, is the address of your website. If you called your company *Cakealicious*, then the perfect URL would be **www.cakealicious.com**. You want it to be memorable, easy to type, and unlikely to result in spelling mistakes. For instance **www.claires-cakealicious-cakes.com** would be just too long and would allow for too many opportunities for customers to make an error when typing. There are thousands of companies who will help you search for and register a domain name. Some of these also offer hosting for websites, e-mail accounts, website building tools and even e-commerce solutions.

Registering your domain name is pretty cheap—it can be as little as $10 a year, and you retain ownership of that domain as long as you pay and renew. If you fail to renew and let it lapse even for a day, someone else could buy it. So it's worth paying for a couple of years up-front, enabling an "auto-renew" feature for your bank account, and making sure your contact details on your account stay up to date so they can send you a renewal reminder. Here are just a few companies to check out:

www.godaddy.com
www.register.com
www.namesecure.com

So before you set your heart on your company name, you should do a web search to see if the best domain name is available. If your first choice domain is available, fantastic, register it quick, and also I'd recommend registering several variations— .com, .net, and so on. This isn't that YOU will necessarily use them – though who knows when you may be ready to expand internationally! It will at least prevent someone else in another country launching a website that your customers may accidentally go to. Especially if they're selling a similar kind of product.

Now it may be that cakealicious.com will come up as "unavailable". Either it has been bought by a company which makes a living from registering millions of domain names in the hope that people just like you will come along and offer to buy one from them, or someone is actually using it for their own business. Quite simply putting the web address into your search bar will reveal all. You will either find a cake company called Cakealicious, or you may find a web company asking you to "make them an offer "!

This has happened to me in the past. Because I was at such an early stage of deciding on the company name, rather than risk paying hundreds or thousands for a URL I didn't absolutely need, I went back to the drawing board and came up with a new company name that I could find the right URL for.

So, deciding on your company name, and getting your Domain Name should really go hand-in-hand!

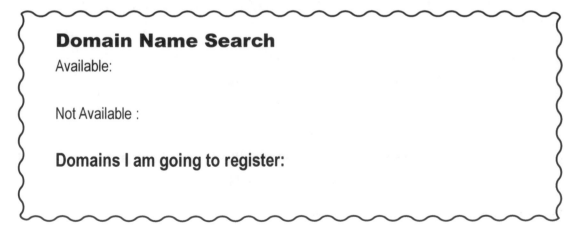

Domain Name Search

Available:

Not Available :

Domains I am going to register:

Choosing A Logo

Pretty much every business you can think of has a logo. Your logo should tie in clearly with the image you want to project for your business. Your logo could be a picture, a graphic symbol, or even just a simple monogram using the key letters of your business name.

Think about your company mission statement and the keywords you feel best describe your business. If you see your business and cakes as fun, quirky, rebellious and alternative, then a bland two letter logo may not best represent you visually. Likewise, if you're specialising in organic ingredients and natural flavours, a cartoon cupcake probably isn't going to send out the right message to your customers either. You want a logo that will reflect your company's personality, products and mission statement, and appeal to the type of customer you feel would buy your cakes—all in one small image. Easy, right?

Whenever I've been stumped for logo ideas, I have a good look around at other companies for inspiration. By looking at logos I loved, and those I wasn't so keen on, I began to form ideas for my own.

Have a look around at other cake companies and start noting and sketching any logos that you love, and think about how they represent that brand.

Inspiration is everywhere

Perhaps you love the way one company uses a clean, simple line drawing of a tiered cake to portray honesty and simplicity. Or how another cleverly uses the shapes of the letters of their company names in combination with a large cake shape. Think about how you could apply that general idea to your own logo.

It goes without saying that there is a big difference between being inspired by another person's logo or website design and out and out ripping it off, so be careful!

What Makes A Great Logo?

Simple

Memorable

Communicates clearly the personality of your business

Works well in both black & white and color

Your Company Colors

Now you may have decided on a simple black and white line drawing for your logo, which is fine. But if you're going for a full color logo, which is preferable, then the colors you will use are just as important as the logo style itself.

Again, think about your products, your "brand", and the colors that best represent your mission statement, as these will be used across your website and brochures as well as on your logo.

Cool Colors

Cool colors tend to have a calming effect. At one end of the spectrum they are cold, impersonal, antiseptic colors. At the other end the cool colors are comforting and nurturing. Blue, green, and the neutrals white, gray, and silver are examples of cool colors. They tend to also give a more sophisticated impression—perfect if you want to specialise in high end classic tiered wedding cakes.

Warm Colors

Warm colors convey emotions from simple optimism to strong violence. The warmth of red, yellow, pink, or orange can create excitement or even anger. The neutrals of black and brown also carry attributes of warm colors.

Metallics

While it may be tempting to opt for silver or gold—particularly if you are focusing on wedding cakes, or wish to portray a luxurious brand image…be aware that this will mean more expensive printing costs on all of your packaging, business cards, flyers etc. Special spot color processes for metallics can be very expensive, and you may soon live to regret your silver logo when it's time to print 5,000 flyers and the cost is double what it could be!

PMS Pantone Colors

No, PMS colors are not the colour of chocolate or wine when you're feeling rather hormonal—PMS stands for Pantone Matching System! Pantones are a standardized ink color system used in the printing industry, to ensure that images and logos are created in exactly the same colors no matter where you choose to have your item printed. So if your logo uses Pantone PMS 1915 (Pink) and PMS 9235 (Blue), then you would quote that to every printer you work with to ensure continuity across all your printed matter.

Colors and their meanings:

Cool Colors

Blue: water, fresh, strong, important, peaceful, intelligent

Turquoise: feminine, sophisticated, retro

Silver: sleek, glamorous, rich

Lavender: graceful, elegance, delicate, feminine

Warm Colors

Red: sexy, hot, love, passion, heat, joy, power

Orange: energy, warmth change, health

Pink: sweet, nice, romance, playful, delicate

Yellow: happy, joy, cheerful, remembrance

Green: organic, healthy, natural, growth, health, environment, harmony

Purple: royal, precious, romantic, sacred, hippy, gothic

Gold: riches, extravagance, traditional

Neutral Colors

Beige: conservative, relaxing

White: clean, classic, purity, innocence, softness

Black: conservative, mysterious, sophisticated, gothic

Grey/Gray: formal, conservative, sophisticated

Ivory: quiet, pleasant, understated elegance

Brown: earthiness, wholesomeness, simplicity, friendliness

Typeface/Font

The typeface you use for your logo and other business literature can communicate a lot about your image, so choose carefully. In addition to those already available on your computer there are plenty available for free download online. If you're using a designer to help with your logo and marketing materials, they will probably already have a great selection to choose from.

Your Logo Ideas:

Have a think about what sort of logo would work best for you. What colors can you visualise? Will it contain a shape or image, or just text?

Colors:

Images or shapes to use:

Sketch some ideas here:

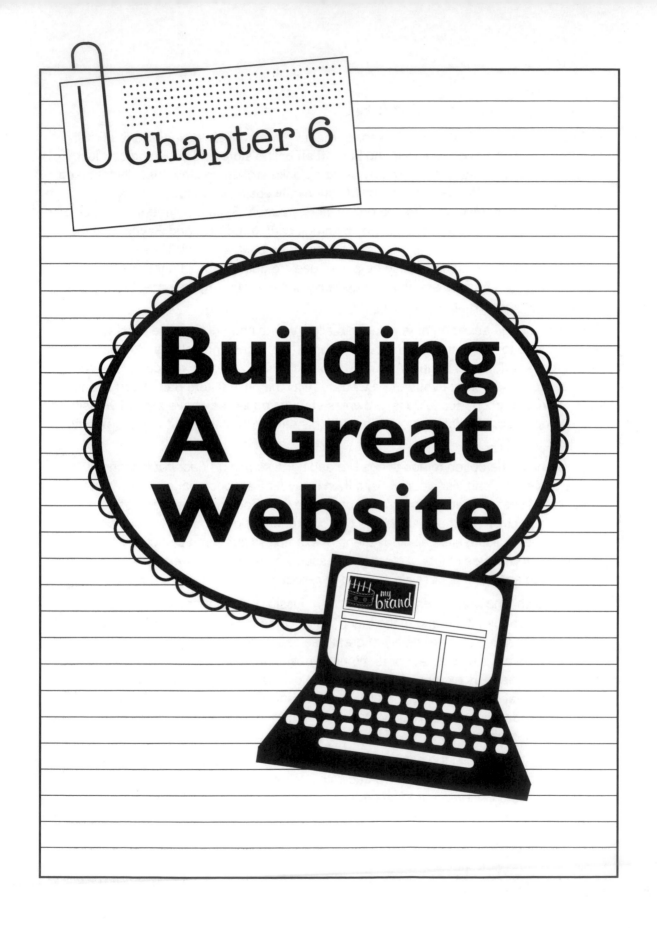

Chapter 6

Building A Great Website

Building a Great Website

Not so long ago, having your own website meant paying a web designer tons of cash to custom design a fancy website and build in an online store and shopping cart just for you. Nowadays, there are so many amazing online resources that, usually for just a small monthly fee, you can not only build your own website, but update, run and manage your very own website and online store yourself. Secure payment processing is all taken care of—customers can pay by credit card, debit card and Paypal and the money (less a transaction fee) goes straight into your bank account. These sites are so user-friendly that you don't need to be a tech geek to get to grips with them—if you can use a computer, chances are you'll be perfectly capable of using their great templates to get your own store up and running.

There are a large selection of templates to allow you to choose the style and layout of your site, and to customise it with your own branding, logos and colours. You have the option to add additional pages (About Us, Contact, Price List etc.) you can also use these templates to create your entire website AND the online store part, if you intend to sell and ship goods (cake pops, brownies etc.). If you already have a great website and decide to add this later on, you can add this new online store part into an existing website easily too.

You also have the option to add things like adding "*Like this on Facebook*" icons, where customers can visit your website then like your Facebook page, or you can post photos of cakes, or special sale promotions, onto your Facebook business page and link them directly to your site so people can click and go right through to your website. Most website building sites also have tons of examples where you can click and view the online stores/sites of lots of other businesses who have used their tools—it's a great way to see what is possible using their resources!

Although with time and patience it's more than possible, building their own website isn't for everybody. At the end of the day it will all come down to your budget and skills. If you can afford it, there are plenty of great freelance website designers out there— many of them are also stay-at-home moms or designers working from home—and it really isn't nearly as expensive as you think. Now that website designers can also use these great site templates, their job is easier and most good designers can work to whatever realistic budget you give them, even if it's only hundreds rather than thousands of dollars.

I've tried both options in the past—I've built one or two very simple sites that only needed to be functional, and I've worked with my amazing designer Julie from '*The Great Little Design Company*' to create sites, logos and flyers that I want to look fantastic. And guess which site looked best?! At the end of the day, we should all play to our strengths and do what we do best.

If funds are low, there may be a friend of a friend out there who will design a simple site and logo for you in exchange for her wedding cake, or next 3 birthday cakes? Always worth bartering and asking around!

Online Store Building Sites

www.shopify.com
www.bigcartel.com
www.bigcommerce.com
www.ekmpowershop.com
www.moonfruit.com
www.volusion.com

"How I Did It"

"I paid a friend who was trained in graphic design to create a logo and then contacted a website company to build the website. It was hard work and a steep learning curve for me but I cannot underline enough the importance of getting yourself a good website that reflects you, your business and portfolio. First impressions count when it comes to most things, websites included. Word of mouth and personal recommendations are still very important, but I think this stands equally alongside having a good website."

Melissa Rayner, Fairy Dust Bakery

What's In a Website?

If you're building a new company website from scratch, you need to create a look and feel that is consistent with your "brand" and all of your other marketing tools and logo. The online site template you have chosen will provide you with details of what size and format your logo or "banner" needs to be—this can either be created by you or your logo designer and inserted into your shop layout. You will then be able to choose the layout from a large selection of themes, and adjust the colour and font of the display to create a website that looks a million dollars!

Here are some of the pages you will then create/add:

Home Page

This is the first page people will land on and should show them, at a glance, what you're all about. It should feature your logo, one or more stunning photos, and a couple of paragraphs outlining what your company is all about. Icons with links to your Facebook and twitter accounts should be on the homepage. Then it's time to add the other pages.

Homepage for 'Georgetown Cupcake': www.georgetowncupcake.com

About Us

Pretty straightforward this one! This is just a small blurb telling your customers all about you, your company and your products. You can use this area to mention your company ethos, or mission statement, and more information about your products, how they are made, the materials or creative process involved. Basically the kind of information that will inspire customers to want to order one of your wonderful creations! This information may already be on your home page, in which case a dedicated About Us page is not strictly necessary.

Homepage for 'The Vanilla Pod Bakery': www.vanillapodbakery.com

Photo Gallery

This is one of **_THE_** most important pages on your website—a chance for you to showcase your talents and range of cakes to all potential customers. In addition to the overall feel of your website, a customer will pretty much decide whether to order from you when viewing your gallery. Also ask your designer to set up your site so that you can easily upload new images yourself, rather than having to keep paying them to update the page. The best Gallery pages:

- **Use bright, clear images**—photo quality is key. Daylight, with a plain background, will show off your cakes in their best light!

- **Show your versatility**—Keep your batteries charged and your camera to hand and be sure to photograph every cake before it leaves your kitchen!

- **Show Cakes In Situ**—After you set up at a wedding, take photos of that stunning cake or cupcake tower—this helps customers visualize their own wedding.

- **Are easy to view**—A slideshow option is ideal. Customers can click on one cake image, then scroll through all the rest. Having to click in and out of every single cake image can be boring and you may lose the customer after half a dozen! See the Resources page for image gallery templates.

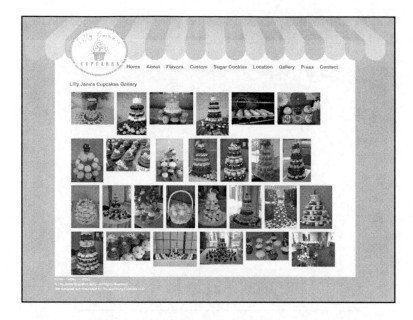

Gallery page for 'Lily Jane's Cupcakes': www.lillyjanescupcakes.com

Gallery page for 'Magnolia Bakery': www.magnoliabakery.com

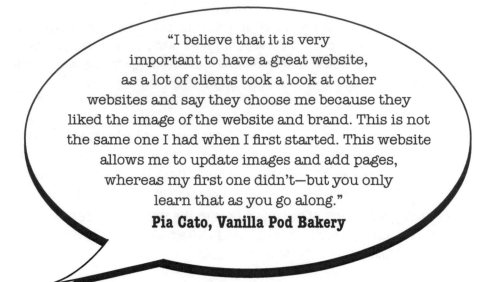

"I believe that it is very important to have a great website, as a lot of clients took a look at other websites and say they choose me because they liked the image of the website and brand. This is not the same one I had when I first started. This website allows me to update images and add pages, whereas my first one didn't—but you only learn that as you go along."

Pia Cato, Vanilla Pod Bakery

Menu/Price List

Even though your cakes may be bespoke and prices obviously vary according to the design, customers like to have an idea of what sort of prices to expect. You should have done your costings and created your price list by now, so look to other sites for inspiration as to how best to present your prices.

Menu page for 'Kakes By Kim': www.kakesbykim.ca

Testimonials

Always a great idea to have some of the great feedback on display, so ask previous customers, if you have any, for a feedback quote—or start asking ask you go along and update the page regularly. If at all possible, have each quote beside a picture of the actual cake—this will make the quote seem even more authentic.

Contact Us

This should include your business phone number and email address for customer enquiries. I would advise against putting your full address (you don't really want people turning up at home unexpectedly!), so something like "*Belinda's Bakery is based from home in Ocoee, Florida and is state registered and insured.*"

You can also state your hours of business next to the phone number, so that customers are encouraged to call between, say 10am–5pm, and won't be surprised to reach voice-mail outside these hours.

More Information

This section should include details of how you intend to do business. If a customer is about to order something from you, this section should contain all the need to know about the ordering process. People like to get as much information as they can up front before calling a company, so try to think of all the things a potential customer may ask, and aim to include them here.

Consultations

Deposits/
Cancellation Policy

Stand Hire

Delivery Charges
and Areas

Payment options

Selling Cakes via Your Website

As well as being a virtual "shop window" for your custom cake business, some cake makers use their website as an online store to sell a selection of suitable baked goods to deliver to customers across the UK. Clearly it's not advisable to ship fragile cakes, or those with buttercream that can be spoiled or bashed, but items like cake pops, cookies and brownies, if wrapped and packed correctly, can survive the postal service.

Cupcakes decorated with fondant and packed correctly can also be mailed on a next-day service. If this is something you're considering, do a google search for "cupcakes delivered" and see what the competition is offering, how they're packaging their baked goods, and what sort of shipping costs are being quoted. Then think carefully about whether you have the resources, or the inclination, to add this to your offerings.

Online orders can come in at any time, so are you equipped to respond to orders immediately—to bake and ship the next working day? What if you have a quiet week with no baking to do until the end of the week for a wedding order, so you have planned a trip away, and an online order for 6 cupcakes comes in on a Sunday evening. Are you willing to drop everything to fulfil this? Ironically, the busier you become, the easier it is to offer online sales as you will most likely be baking each day anyway, so perhaps this is a section of your business that you will look to add on in later months?

"Probably 40% of my business is online ordering, though I think a lot of people still like having a conversation and a personable approach.
**Kathryn Carter,
The Kooky Cake Company**

If you do want to add an Online Store section to your website, again you can use one of the Shopping Cart/template sites—several are featured on the Resources page at the back of the book. Your website designer, or you, can easily add in this additional page and make it blend with the rest of your website.

Product Categories

It's time to start adding your products! First up, jot down the various categories you need to cover. i.e Gift Boxes, Cupcakes, Cookies, Cake Pops. Then any sub-categories within each: mini cupcakes/regular cupcakes, gluten free cookies etc.

Main Category: Cupcakes> Regular Cupcakes/ Mini Cupcakes

You can also allocate each product into several categories, so that it will show up in each relevant category. For instance a Gift Box of 6/9/12 cupcakes would be in both the Gift Box and the Cupcake categories.

Obviously, you don't want to over-complicate things and make your customer jump through various hoops to find something, but choosing logical categories, and including the correct products in each, can make the browsing experience much simpler for your customers.

Product Descriptions

This should be a clear and concise description of your cakes/products, giving the customer all the information they need to decide if this is the right item for them. Because a customer buying online can't touch, feel, smell or taste your product, it's important that they know enough from your Product Description and photo to confidently go ahead and make that purchase. As well as an overall description, be sure to add more details like flavour and colour options, ingredients etc.

Flavor Options (cake and toppings)

Your store template should also allow you at this stage to create drop down choices to allow you to list all the cake options and frosting options available. So your mini cupcakes are available in either vanilla, red velvet or chocolate fudge cake options, you can create these as a drop down box. Likewise frosting/icing colours or flavors. Or if you have set combinations options could be chocolate/vanilla, red velvet/cream cheese etc.

Price

Again, your template will show you where to add in the price for each item, and if you have price variations for each flavor, size or topping you can add that in too.

Customer Comments

A customer may wish to draw your attention, or give you information like the name of the recipient, or the initial to go on each cupcake.

Discount Codes

These can be a great promotional tool. Having a Valentine's Special Menu and about to do a Newsletter offering your subscribers or Facebook fans 20% off certain, or selected, goods, or Free Shipping if they spend a certain amount? No problem, you can set up a Discount Code to give out to customers, and set the parameters like expiry date, what it can be used for and how many times, and in conjunction with any other discounts etc. Customers will enter this at the checkout to receive their discount. It can take a while to get the hang of using these extra features.

Other Features

Each online store template provider will vary, but here are more great features you can enjoy when building your online store.

Similar Items

"*If you like this, you may also like these*"—show similar items at the foot of the page of a particular product.

Customer communication

Click and the software automatically generates updates like "*your order is being processed/has shipped*" emails to your customers as you pack and ship each order.

Shipping Prices

Shipping can be calculated by product, by value, by postal area, by weight, and various other methods. Research the true cost of shipping your products before you set your shipping prices.

Social Networking

With some shopping cart software you can even add "share/like" buttons next to each actual product, so that customers can post on their Facebook pages that they "*like*" your Cupcake Birthday Box!

Sales Reports

Click to check your sales by date, product—see what are your busy months, which products are selling best, what impact each discount code has had etc.

Service With A Smile!

One of the great things about selling directly to the public—especially something as fun and well-loved as cakes—can be the personal interaction with people. Nothing is more rewarding than an email from a satisfied customer, or some great feedback left on your website praising your wonderful cake designs or service. But, as the old saying goes "*Happy customers tell 3 friends, unhappy ones tell 300*", when the customer is less than satisfied it can feel like the worst thing that's ever happened.

Rule Number 1 is to treat the customer as you would like to be treated yourself. If I emailed a website with a quick question about an item and didn't receive a response for 3 or 4 days, not only would I assume that they're not going to be the most professional or efficient outfit around, but it may even make me question whether to go ahead and order from them. Will I ever get the goods? Will they be well made or well packaged? Or will I be chasing this person for weeks on end wondering where my goods are?

Communication is king!
Always respond to your customers as quickly as possible, ideally within 24 hours. If you're going to be away for more than a day at a fair, or on holiday, set up an email auto-reply stating that. Or better still, can you check your emails each evening wherever you are, or have them on your phone and send a quick reply when you can?

Keep the customer involved in each step of their order process…
…and they will feel happy in the knowledge that their purchase is being dealt with. Confirm when an order has been received. Let them know when they can expect to receive their order. Inform them immediately of any delays, giving them the option to cancel if the delay means they no longer need the item.

Once the item has been received, consider a follow-up email.
Check if they are happy with their purchase, thank them for their custom, offer a discount on their next visit. You could even, on this email, invite them to subscribe to your newsletter or "*like*" you on Facebook.

Thank you!

Customer Communication Rules

Reply promptly, ideally within 24 hours, to ALL feedback.

Treat the customer as you would like to be treated

Leave your emotions at home (or at least in the other room!)

Remain professional at all times

Communication is King!

Say Thank You!

Nice Touch!

The great thing about being a small business owner is that we have the freedom and flexibility to add the personal touches in our business dealings that large corporations can't. We can provide a genuinely human connection and create a pleasant experience for our customers, and add in those little touches that can make the experience more special for them.

It really is the little things that make a difference. Think about how you package and ship your orders. Could you use a cuter box, and wrap them in pretty tissue paper, sealed with a cool logo sticker? How about a hand-written note, wishing your customer lots of fun and enjoyment on their special day? I have a pin-board full of cute business cards and postcards, with lovely messages that remind me of past gifts and purchases, and I often refer back to them and return to those online stores as I know that the owner genuinely appreciates my business. Stickers or refrigerator magnets with "*I Love Cake*" and your website address at the bottom are cute, cheap and could be included in every order.

Or how about including a couple of beautifully wrapped cake pops in with every order—a great way to show your customers what else you offer, and these lovely little touches will keep them coming back again and again.

So—have a think about how you can go that extra mile for your customers and make their day!

Chapter 7

Marketing & PR

NEWS

Marketing and PR are the essential tools in making your potential customers aware that you exist! You could have the best tasting and most stunningly beautiful cakes in the world, but unless people know about you, you might never get a single order!

Whether or not you think you already have the skills to become a successful "marketeer", if you're passionate about your cakes, and want to sell as many of them as possible, then so many aspects of "marketing and pr" will be things that you instinctively want to do anyway. If you love what you do, and are proud of the cakes that you're creating, why wouldn't you want to shout it from the rooftops?

I personally never leave the house without a stack of business cards in my bag—and when I was launching my business I quickly distributed over 5,000 flyers—with the help of family and friends—and literally walked the streets spreading the word, such was my passion and determination to make a success of my new venture!

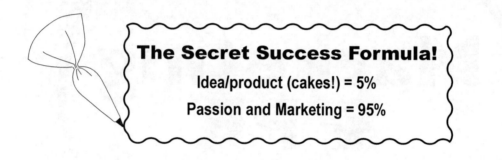

The Secret Success Formula!

Idea/product (cakes!) = 5%

Passion and Marketing = 95%

A good Marketing and PR campaign will identify the type of people you want to reach, and find both obvious and inventive ways of reaching them. While large companies have equally large marketing budgets, the smaller company or entrepreneur must look to find ways to reach their customers that is cost effective and within their limited budget.

The ultimate aim is obviously to sell your cakes and take lots of good orders. Unless you have an unlimited budget to throw at paid advertising, you'll need to have a "think outside the box" attitude—and plenty of determination. You need to approach a broad range of people to let them know all about your new company and fabulous cakes—and about you too! No time to become a shrinking violet, sometimes you may find that the local paper is interested in running a story about a new, local company like yours, with the entire article based around you...they love the human angle!!

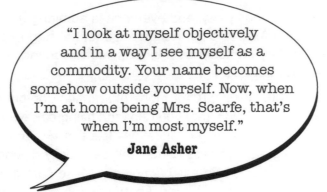

"I look at myself objectively and in a way I see myself as a commodity. Your name becomes somehow outside yourself. Now, when I'm at home being Mrs. Scarfe, that's when I'm most myself."

Jane Asher

Marketing

This involves the use of advertisements, brochures, flyers, newsletters and other profile-raising means to reach your customers.

PR

Public Relations covers the use of the media to make your customers aware of your product or service. Magazines, newspapers, TV and radio (both national and local) are all key ways of gaining exposure.

Online PR and Social Networking

The use of Facebook, twitter, blogs and websites to reach potential customers. The opportunities to promote yourself and your products online are endless, with a worldwide reach! In fact, such is the power of Social Networking that I've dedicated the whole of **Chapter 8** to Social Media and Online PR!

Marketing and PR Tools

Your Marketing & PR Tool Kit

Business cards

Quality Product Photos

Brochure/Flyer

Online presence (Website, Chapter 6)

Business Cards

So you're at a friend's birthday party, and everyone is admiring the wonderful cakes you brought along. Your friend tells her neighbor about her hugely talented friend… and it so happens that the neighbor has a birthday party coming up too, or a niece who is planning her wedding.

She asks if you have a business card, or more information on your cakes and how to contact you. Well, do you? Now that you're a high flying cakey entrepreneur, you'll hopefully find yourself in plenty of situations like this. So you should definitely arm yourself with some great business cards. You can easily design them yourself, or there are tons of online tools with easy templates. Make sure the design and feel of your business cards fit in with your overall branding too and features your logo, email and contact phone number. You can even consider featuring an image of your cakes on the reverse. My favourite new site for business cards is **www.moo.com**. You can choose from hundreds of cool images, funky rounded corner style cards, recycled paper, or even upload your own images so that your business cards feature your very own cakes! Feel free to go crazy and order a few hundred, after all, you'll soon be networking like mad, right?

Quality Product Images

As you know from the previous chapter you will need a great selection of cake photos for your new website. As well as your website, you should have at least half a dozen great images ready to provide to any local magazines or newspapers that may want to feature you.

These should include a couple of shots of you, with your cakes. Not all local magazines or newspapers have the budget to send a photographer along to take photos—but if you can supply them with great images as well as a great story, then it will be much easier to convince them to write about you!

Get an apron printed with your logo and website displayed prominently at chest level. Make sure you wear this in every photo, and at any events you do. That way, if a newspaper should forget to mention your business name you still get your website and brand out there (believe me this happens, you could spend ages arranging a feature and all it says is "*local cake-maker Jane Green*" with no contact info! So make sure to cover all bases.)

Most publications will only use images that are high resolution—usually 300dpi or higher. DPI ('Dots Per Inch') is the industry standard for printing, and 300dpi is the most used as it allows photos within magazines or brochures to be printed clearly. You will also need 300 dpi images in order to create a lovely colour flyer or brochure. So make sure your photographer knows this, or set your digital camera to the highest quality setting.

Once you have your high–resolution photos, you may see that, because they are such high quality, each photo could be a file size of 3 or 4 MB each. Such large files take ages to upload to your online store or website—websites don't need images at such high quality, and in fact some online store templates won't allow you to upload images of any more than 500kb (half a MB) as it takes up too much server space.

I like to shoot all my images as high-res, so that I have every image as high a quality as possible for press and brochures, then I create a new set of low resolution ones for using on websites or emailing for people to view first. You can do this easily at sites like **www.shrinkpictures.com.**

You upload the high-res shot then choose to save it at a much lower file size. I then use these lower resolution images to send to people, or to drop into press releases or use on the website—they can still be viewed on their computer perfectly clearly but without the enormous file size of the high-res ones!

Taking Great Cake Photos

• Use plain, simple backgrounds—people need to see the cakes, not the background

• Use natural light, as flash can distort the colours

• Take photos from several different angles to see what works best

• Take close-up shots of any key details or features of a cake, like intricate piping details

• Avoid shadows or direct lighting

• Make sure you have that one clear, bright, killer shot of each cake

• Make sure you shoot in high resolution—300dpi is required for most printing

• Never send lots of high-res attachments by email without checking with recipient first!

Creating a Great Flyer or Brochure

Now that you're all set up as a proper business, you'll need some stunning flyers to give out to new and prospective customers.

You can get 5,000 full color double-sided A5 flyers printed for as little as $70—this may sound like a lot of flyers, but with the economies of scale, ordering 5000 is not much pricier than 1000. These flyers are also cheap enough to give away and use for lots of local marketing ideas – more of which later—so you can easily commit to a decent print run, safe in the knowledge that you'll soon use them up spreading the word! (See **Resources** for suggested printing websites, or try Google.)

Because you will have a great website that customers can go to for more detailed information, you just need something simple—that looks great—to give out to customers at school fairs and in your local area to show them your great cakes and encourage them to call or visit your website for more info.

One side of your flyer should feature your logo at the top, and the website and business phone number across the bottom, a short blurb about your cake company, and, most importantly some fantastic cake photos. You could use the rear of the flyer to show off lots of different cake images.

Don't be tempted to clutter up the flyer with prices, email addresses and too much info. If people can get online, they will go to your website. If they can't, they can call you. Keep it fresh, clean and simple—the cakes should be the stars!

Unless you're already a design whizz, this is where you may need to spend some cash having your flyer professionally designed. Remember, this will be your main "marketing tool", so it's important that you take the time to produce something really special.

Deciding where to distribute your flyers is when you need to be as lateral in your thinking as possible. Think of places where people visit and spend time in your local area…some examples are:

Come Fly(er) With Me!!

- Doctors surgery
- Dentists surgery
- Local kids activity venues
- Libraries
- Coffee shop noticeboards
- Grocery store noticeboards
- Kids judo/karate venues
- Gyms/health clubs/leisure centres/swimming pools
- Yoga studios
- Children's party, soft play and activity type venues
- Veterinary surgery
- Toy stores
- Childrens clothes stores
- Beauty salons/nail salons/spas/alternative therapy centres
- Bookstores
- Church hall noticeboards
- Venues for girls scouts
- Food takeaway places—waiting areas where people have time to sit and notice flyers!
- Ask your kid's school if you can put a flyer in each of the kids' book bags. In exchange for this, you could offer to do a cake or cookie decorating session for a class, or a competition for one mom to win a birthday cake!

Using flyers and posters in your local area is a cheap and effective way to reach potential customers. It may take lots of leg work, but it can be worth the effort. Always keep a bundle in your bag as when you're "off duty" and popping to the grocery store you may spot a gap in the noticeboard that's perfect for your flyer!

Local companies

Are there any large companies in your area? Why not pop into reception and ask if you can either leave some flyers on reception, or whether they have a staff "intranet" or website that features ads or info? You could even offer a special staff discount code! Or how about delivering a box of 24 cupcakes, with a load of your cards or flyers attached—now that will really get their attention!

Not only could the company itself start ordering from you for parties, special meetings, or leaving parties, but there are hundreds of staff that could be ordering from you for their own special occasions.

Local Events: Is there an annual Fourth Of July parade, carnival, fireworks display, funfair or Christmas Fair in your area? Or how about local school events—sports games, homecoming parades etc. If so, these can be cheap and effective ways to promote your business—how about taking a stall selling affordable cupcakes or cookies for kids to buy, while you hand out flyers to the parents. Creating and giving out cool stickers with "*I Love Cake*" (or something fun) and your website address on them will be devoured by kids…give one to every child. Next time mom is thinking of ordering a special cake—guess which local company will spring to mind?

Approaching Magazines and Newspapers

Getting featured in magazines and newspapers is the holy grail of every small business person! Not only is it FREE, but it's been proven time and again that editorial content has hugely more impact on sales than any paid advertising could even hope to achieve. With a bit of luck and a lot of perseverance soon you could soon be spotting you and your cakes on the pages of your local paper or magazines!

Local Press

You already live in your area so you should be familiar with any local magazines or newspapers. These publications are always keen to feature local people doing interesting things, so you could pitch them a feature about your new company launch. Even better, give them a "hook to hang it on" like the fact that you are selling your cakes at a forthcoming local event—that way readers will be encouraged to come along and visit your booth or table. Or offer them a reader competition—guess how many sprinkles are on the giant cupcake in the photo (that you will provide them with, and you will be standing behind the cupcake with your logo-d apron on!)

These journalists are an important part of ensuring your local profile, so it's vital to strike up a great working relationship with them.

Don't be intimidated at the thought of approaching journalists—remember, these people WANT to write about interesting local people, that's their job! It's *your* job to convince them that, out of the hundreds of other options, they should write about *YOU*!

As well as local papers, do you have any "*What's On*" type magazines, or those aimed at parent's and families? Or what about those glossy lifestyle magazines that are often distributed through local upmarket bars and boutiques? Start looking, I bet there are many more opportunities for PR than you first thought!

Sending a box of delicious cupcakes along with a press release and flyer to the right person at a magazine or newspaper can work wonders, and is well worth the time and effort!

Other PR Opportunities

TV & Radio

If you have an event coming up, this could be the perfect time to gain some valuable local TV or Radio coverage.

Call up your local Radio station and even the local, regional TV news program to find out the contact details for the Producer or Researcher for that show. Email brief information of what you're up to, then follow it up with a call.

You can even try calling up a local radio quiz show—they always have a chat about what you do—as this gives a sneaky opportunity to get your info across—don't forget to mention your website as soon as you can, as it's the one thing people remember!

Cover your car!

Did you know that having your business logo and information splashed all over your car isn't as expensive as you think? For a few hundred dollars you can have your car "wrapped" or vinyl applied to make your car a 24/7 advert for your company! Imagine a huge cupcake on your bonnet, with more cakes, your logo, website and phone number and "*Custom Cakes across Orlando*" splashed on the side of each car…now that's going to catch people's eyes! Even as you go about your daily business—school run, trip to the supermarket, trek to Ikea, you are marketing your cake company to the whole area, with no effort! It's a no-brainer!

Most companies will do the design for you, tailored exactly to your vehicle, as part of the price. An investment that could pay for itself a hundred times over!

Custom Car Sun Shades

If you're not quite ready for the cost or commitment of covering your whole car, how about a custom sunshade—get your message across and advertise the business at the traffic lights, in supermarket car parks, and wherever people are close to your car. A great low-cost alternative.

Marketing & PR Checklist

Have you done absolutely everything to market your business?

Created a list of local
papers and magazines

Contacted journalists

Followed up at least once

Considered Local TV & Radio

Created and ordered flyers
for local distribution

Started handing out flyers
locally at every opportunity!

Asked all local schools about
book bags and school fairs

Approached all local businesses,
dropped of flyers and/or cakes

Roped in family and friends
to help distribute flyers too!

Chapter 8

Social Networking & Online PR

Using Social Media for your Business

Word-of-mouth marketing has long been the most effective sales too of all for businesses of all sizes. Why? Because we trust the recommendations of friends and family way more than any slick advert or glossy marketing brochure. When a friend says something is good—whether it's their mechanic, a local pizzeria, or an amazing cake they had made for a bridal shower—you trust their opinion!

These days, social media takes all the innate benefits of word-of-mouth marketing, and adds to it the capacity to reach thousands (or even millions) of people. Not only do we tend to share the same likes and interests as other members of our social networks, but we also tend to ask these people for advice on where to go, shop, eat, stay and play.

Developing a strong online presence is key to any new business these days—and the great news is it's can be the cheapest and most effective form of marketing you will ever do. With just a little time and continued effort, the use of the likes of Facebook, Twitter, newsletters and even starting a blog can pay huge dividends. Here's how to get started!

Facebook

Facebook is not just for keeping tabs on friends and sharing your latest holiday snaps—it can also be used as a highly effective business tool. It's great for marketing your products and connecting with your customers. If you're just starting your social media marketing campaign, Facebook is most likely where you need to be. All you need is to create a "Fan Page" for your business, and you're all set!

Creating a Facebook fan page is a straightforward process, but you do need to have the following things before you begin:

1. A Personal Facebook Account

"Why does Facebook require I set-up my business account through my PERSONAL account!"—this is one of the big questions people who start the process of creating their business Fan Pages ask—and believe me, I also wondered this myself at first.

Think of your personal credentials as your "badge" that you swipe every time you enter through the virtual gates of Facebook. Facebook's Terms of Service require that you use your real name & info—and your use of the features of the site (Fan Pages included,) are dependent on your agreeing to abide by Facebook's rules & regulations. Everything you create (photos, groups, Fan Pages,) are done by YOU, the real person. But, that does not mean that users of your business fan page will be able to access your personal info, be your friend, or even know it was you that created the page. Phew!

To sum it up—like it or not, you will need to have a personal profile in order to create a fan page for your business. Chances are you're probably one of the 800 million people out there already signed up to Facebook anyway!

2. Here's The Link to Create A Fan Page!

Go to any page that you are already a fan ("liker") of and scroll down towards the bottom of the page while keeping an eye on the left column. By doing this you may eventually see a link to "*Create a Page*". Or you can just use this handy link!

http://www.facebook.com/pages/create.php

3. A Good Name

Hint: it is extremely difficult (bordering on impossible) to change your page's name once you've made the decision. Other things can be changed fairly easily—but the name is here to stay.

For some businesses, this will be pretty obvious (the name of your business for instance), but take a second to think about your name, make sure you're spelling it correctly (seriously, this happens) and do a quick search just to double check there isn't another FB group out there with the same, or very similar, name.

4. Branding & Other Info

The rest of the "customisation" of your Facebook Fan Page is fairly straightforward. While there are options for further customisation (custom tabs) Facebook keeps a fairly standard look throughout the site & its many pages. Options you have for customisation include: a profile image, info about your business, and the option to direct first-time visitors to a unique page.

Your profile picture will appear on the page and also as a thumbnail for all posts you make. In considering your business page profile picture—I would encourage you to consider your overall branding efforts. If you have a logo—use it! You may have to modify it for FB purposes (to ensure it isn't cut-off in the thumbnail) but you want to maintain consistent branding throughout your social media efforts. Also, once you've selected a profile/thumbnail image—don't change it (or at least, change it VERY rarely!) Your logo will become visually associated with the content you're sharing in the newsfeed.

Your information is fairly straightforward. Be sure to include your website address and contact email. A brief blurb about WHO your business is and WHAT you do, and WHERE you do it i.e what area you cover. Facebook doesn't give you much room to wax poetic, so get the main points across, so that without even visiting your website potential customers can see the great cakes you do, and how to contact you.

In the "Permissions" section of your page editing options—you can select what Facebook calls a "default tab." This is where your first-time visitors will be directed (all fans will be directed to the "wall" view of your page). You can select: wall, info, photos, videos…and as you add different "apps" to your page, you can add these too. This is how some pages achieve a more "customized" look. A customized welcome tab can truly help set you apart—but you may want to focus on building an audience before you worry too much about more time-intensive design options (though you can pay a company to create a custom tab for you —including us).

5. Add TONS of photos to your photo gallery!

This is where Facebook is really great—you can use it as a virtual shop window for your business and showcase the hundreds of lovely cakes you offer. Check out other Cake businesses on Facebook to see just how well they use photos on their pages . Posting regular, gorgeous photos encourages your fans to comment and admire…all of this can lead to new customers and new orders.

6. Fans Are People who "*Like*" Your Business

Fan pages now have "*likers*" instead of fans. Once your business page is set up, you will need to have fans/likers in order to have any impact at all.

So, how do you generate them? Well…the first thing to keep in mind is that quality trumps quantity any day of the week. Focus on getting people that are truly interested in your product, service, or information. How do you do that? Here are a few helpful hints:

- Take advantage of the "suggest to friends" option under your profile image (on the business page). This gives you the opportunity to share your page with your current (personal) FB friends. I mean, if friends and family don't support your endeavours, who will?

- Integrate Facebook into your website. You can do this by using Facebook's own "developer toolkit." We recommend the "like badge" and also integrating "like" buttons. You can do this if you have access to HTML on your site (or know someone who does).

- Mention your Facebook page in your other marketing materials. This means everything from email signatures, to email marketing campaigns, to business cards. Let people know! Your business card or flyers could include "follow us on Facebook for specials offers, discounts and news".

And there you go. That's the basics of a creating a Facebook page for your business!

Twitter

Several years ago when I first heard about Twitter—a tool for instantly broadcasting the minutiae of your day and following the trifles of others—I couldn't imagine a bigger waste of time. Why would anyone care about what I had for lunch, or whether someone was headed off to the gym? Why would any business person want to get involved in such an obviously social platform?

Well, how wrong I was. Twitter is now used as a key business tool, and developing a Twitter following is now seen as a key part of any business marketing strategy.

How Does Twitter Work?

Twitter users—often called *Tweeple* (or worse)—have 140 characters to answer the question, "*What are you doing*?" If you join Twitter you can "follow" other tweeple, which causes their updates to appear on your home page. In turn, they can follow you. You can also direct message them, but always in 140 characters or less. Twitter communications can be viewed and updated on the Web, through desktop apps, and on mobile devices. In fact, such is the ease with which people can update and view their Twitter profile from their mobile phone, as a business-owner you have the ability to update and connect with your followers and customers literally in the palm of your hand!

How Does Twitter Help You Work?

Within this participating audience of exhibitionists are a growing number of people who are using Twitter for business. From large corporations to crafty entrepreneurs just like yourself, business owners in all corners of the globe are using Twitter as a communications and marketing tool.

Here's how you might use Twitter for your business:

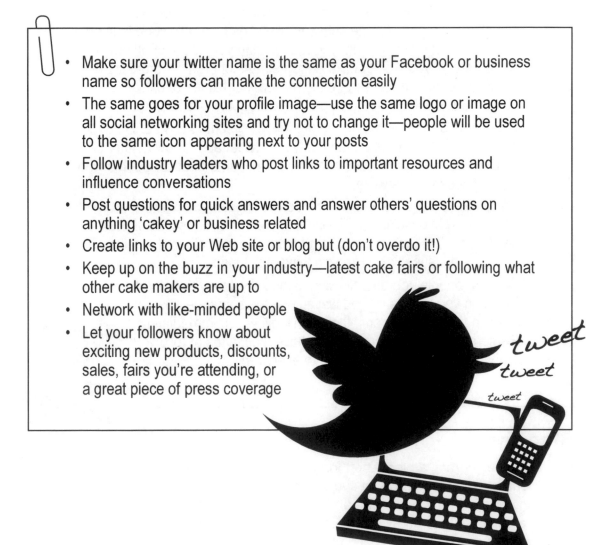

- Make sure your twitter name is the same as your Facebook or business name so followers can make the connection easily
- The same goes for your profile image—use the same logo or image on all social networking sites and try not to change it—people will be used to the same icon appearing next to your posts
- Follow industry leaders who post links to important resources and influence conversations
- Post questions for quick answers and answer others' questions on anything 'cakey' or business related
- Create links to your Web site or blog but (don't overdo it!)
- Keep up on the buzz in your industry—latest cake fairs or following what other cake makers are up to
- Network with like-minded people
- Let your followers know about exciting new products, discounts, sales, fairs you're attending, or a great piece of press coverage

How to Get People to Follow You On Twitter

The more people who follow you on Twitter, the more influence and networking opportunities you have. Thus, it makes sense to try and build a following.

Here are some ideas on getting others to follow you:

- Follow them. There's an almost kneejerk reaction to follow people who follow you. However, there's a backlash against people who follow just about everyone for the sole purpose of gaining followers. In short, be discriminating with whom you follow. Align yourself with others in the same field as you—other cake entrepreneurs or creative organizations like Sugarcraft companies or cake related magazines or exhibition companies, or simply creative people whose work you admire.

- Post some good tweets right before following someone else. I find that if someone follows me and they only tweet about how hungry or tired they are, I don't follow them back. The same goes for people who haven't tweeted in a while.

- Complete your bio. People rarely follow strangers, so complete your one-line bio and include a URL in the More Info URL section of your profile. I can't tell you the number of times I've not bothered to follow someone because I didn't know a thing about them.

- Reply to people you are following, especially if they're not yet following you. That's a good way to engage someone and get them to follow you, even if they didn't follow you immediately. Remember, though, some people have thousands of followers, and may not be able to respond to every reply.

Blogging

Like an online journal, a blog (short for 'web-log', by the way!) is a place to share your thoughts and knowledge on subjects related to your business, create links to useful information, and post news and other announcements. You can use a blog to give a personal face and voice to your business, and include interesting things that are going on in your life in general as well as the business, and create a useful resource your customers will want to revisit often. Blogs can also help you build your professional reputation and gain your customers' trust.

You can easily set up a blog for free, but they're not for everyone. Developing and updating your blog will require an investment of both time and thought, so before you get started, consider whether you can stick to a regular update schedule.

You'll want to update your blog at least once each week: Keeping your content fresh will help show your readers that you're serious about your business. Your posts don't have to be long, but you'll want to keep them interesting news and comments.

Make a schedule for yourself, and dedicate time each week for brainstorming, researching article ideas, and writing your posts.

How Do I Start Blogging?
Well the great news is, starting your own blog doesn't even have to cost you a penny! There are tons of companies out there offering free easy to use build your own blog templates and, with just a little bit of effort and smidgeon of technical savvy, you could have your own beautiful blog up and running in just a few hours ! If you already have a website for your business, your blog can be added to that, or have a link on the website to direct visitors to your blog.

Some of the best blog platform providers have so many useful tools to use—from widgets that you can place on your blog to link your readers right through to your Facebook or Twitter pages, so a Statistics bar that will allow you to check the traffic to your blog, where your readers are coming from and even what search words they used to find you. How cool is that?!

Blog Building Tools

www.wordpress.org

www.typepad.com

www.blogger.com

Branding Your Blog
Just like your website, the look and feel of your blog should reflect your personal and business style. Most of the blog templates available allow you to customize the design, adding in your logo or a banner and choosing the colours, layout and font that work best for you. Take some time to get this right as your blog really is an

extension of your business . Think of it as another marketing tool and give it the same care and attention as you would if you were creating a flyer or brochure.

What Should I Write About?

The thought of sharing your hopes, dreams, plans and schemes with the world can be a little daunting at first: "*What if I don't have anything interesting to say? What if I'm not funny/entertaining/witty/engaging? What on earth will I find to write about every day/week/month?*"

The most important thing is to be yourself. If you're trying too hard to be something you're not, people can tell. Think of it as like being at a party where you don't know anyone. Yes, you do need to make some sort of an effort to be interesting and engaging and get to know people, but if you "try too hard" to be the life and soul of the party and that's not your natural character, then you'll just feel fake and a bit silly! If you speak honestly and from the heart, chances are what you have to say will be engaging and of interest to at least some people.

What you decide to share with your readers is entirely up to you. For some kinds of business blogs, maybe for more formal organizations, it may not be the best idea for the blogger to discuss his personal life—his readers may only be interested in the latest technical or financial information. But as a creative business owner, you and your cake business life are one and the same, and the kind of readers you attract are likely to also be creative individuals who are happy to share in your everyday trials and tribulations.

They'll enjoy hearing about your latest '*cake-tastrophe*', and laugh at photos of your collapsing castle cake, just as much as they will be wowed by photos of your latest 5-tier wedding cake!

Now that doesn't mean posting daily blogs about your efforts to potty-train your 2 year old, but topics such as juggling your son's sports day with getting an order for 144 custom cupcakes ready, or moving home while trying to finish 3 wedding cake orders can give readers a cool insight into your work/life balance!

Photos are a key part of creating a visually interesting blog, and can be a great way to really promote your business too.

Blog Tips

- Post photos of you at work in your kitchen, creating your latest cakes

- Are you attending any events like wedding fairs, trade shows etc? A perfect opportunity to share the journey and pics on your blog!

- Why not run a competition on your Facebook, twitter, blog and website for previous customers to send in photos of them eating/with your cakes. Offer a prize for the funniest/coolest pic. This gives you tons of great photos showing off your products in multiple settings!

- If you're an expert at making something in particular, an online tutorial can be a great way to find new fans and bring traffic to your blog and website. Check out You Tube for ideas from other cake makers out there.

The Final Word on Social Media

While all of the above may look like lots of work, using social media to market your business could be the best thing you ever do. Even if you start with just one, a Facebook page, you'll soon see results and be bitten by the social media bug!

When you compare the cost of just one print advert in a glossy magazine, or mailing out thousands of brochures or flyers, to what can be achieved and the amount of people you can reach using social media for FREE, you'll quickly realize that taking the time to set your business up for social media marketing could be the smartest thing you do for your business.

So go on, get yourself out there and start (social) networking!

Chapter 9

Customers & Orders

ORDER BOOK

Customer Consultations

So now that you're all set up in business, have done tons of networking and marketing and really put the word out there, it's time for the orders to start rolling in! Customers, especially those ordering wedding cakes, will want to have a consultation with you to discuss their requirements, taste your cakes, and decide whether you are the person they'd like to make the cake for the biggest day of their life!

In Chapter 2 we talked about how important it is to have a clean, tidy dedicated area of your home to hold consultations—a visit to your home may be the first impression a customer has and it's crucial that your surroundings reassure them that their cake will be made in a clean, organized and safe environment. Your home is now an extension of your "brand"!

Understandably, some cake bakers—particularly those with small children and a busy family life—are hesitant about holding consultations at home. Some do visit the customer, or meet them in a neutral place like a café or hotel lounge, but from my experience most customers ordering from a home-based baker like to view where their cakes are being made, for their own peace of mind.

Unless you are lucky enough to have a dedicated spare room that you can dress and use only for cake customers, if you will be holding meetings at your kitchen or dining room table it can mean extra work having a massive tidy-up and clean before each customer arrives.

By holding ad-hoc consultations, not only can it eat into family time, it also means baking lots of samples for each and every meeting—very time consuming.

By scheduling a couple of days a month for consultations, not only can you maximize your time by booking them back to back, you can also prepare a batch of samples for tastings that will all be used on the same day—a much better use of your time!

- Hold all consultations on regular, scheduled dates i.e. every second Weds evening.
- Allow plenty of time—1 hour per meeting and a 15 minute gap in between for latecomers!
- Have all your prices, order forms and samples ready so that the customer can make the booking and sign off on their order before they leave.

"Customers come to me for wedding cake consultations or I have gone to their homes. I think they like coming to me so they can see what the kitchen is like and make sure everything is clean etc. They normally come and have a coffee and cake and we chat through ideas. I am very proud that every consultation for a wedding cake that I have had, they have booked their cake with me!"

Kathryn Carter, The Kooky Cake Company

"It is a constant challenge to keep a clean and tidy kitchen when you have children, and especially so when you run a cake business from home too. Most of my work is done during school hours and evenings for this very reason, but I won't deny it can be a source of frustration at times, especially during the weekend when I am often at my busiest! Customers regularly come and collect cakes and I hold consultations for wedding bookings. Cakes are collected at all times of the day, and I always make sure I have finished clearing up and washing up before the customer arrives. Likewise, with wedding consultations, I hold these in the evenings when my children are in bed and the house is calm and tidy!"

Melissa Rayner, Fairy Dust Bakery

Forms & Formalities

Once you and the customer have agreed on a price and the details of their cake, it's time to put everything in writing, and there will be several forms to be completed across the entire process—from Order through to Delivery.

Your Order Form will contain the information on the cake itself, plus the financial details—cake price, deposit amount, balance due date, plus details and costs of any equipment rental and/or delivery charges.

On a separate sheet will be your detailed Terms & Conditions, which you should run through with the customer as they are agreeing to these when they sign each form. These T&C's form the legal contract between yourself and the customer and are there both to protect you and to ensure that both parties are clear on what to expect. Taking the time to go through these will help avoid any misunderstandings as things progress.

A few other forms will be required to ensure everyone has all the information they need *AFTER* the cake is made, so that delivery runs smoothly, and staff at the venue have all the information they need about the cake, like portion cutting guides and any allergy details in case a guest asks.

Forms include:

Order Form (with T&C)	☐
Invoice	☐
Hire Agreement	☐
Delivery/Set-Up Details	☐
Portion/Cutting Guide	☐
Important Cake Information & Allergy information	☐

Later in this chapter are some templates to give you an idea of what to include on your forms, so let's look at what each form should include in more detail.

Order Forms and Deposits

This is the first form to be completed, usually at the time of ordering. Many brides will be happy to get this done at the consultation, once they have decided to go with you. With so much to organise, often they are keen to get this first piece of paperwork done there and then rather than follow up by post. Points to cover on your Order Form are:

- Price of cake, plus any additional costs (delivery/hire etc.)
- Total cost
- Deposit amount
- Balance Due and Date Due
- Cancellations and refunds
- Cake details: Size, dimensions, tiers, cake flavor(s), filling flavors(s), frosting/fondant color(s)
- Decoration details and exact accent colors
- Decorations to be provided by the bride—details
- Sketch of cake
- Alterations
- Viewing
- Allergies/special ingredients
- Collection/Delivery/Set-up

If the bride needs to provide you with anything—specific decorations or a piece of fabric or ribbon for you to colour match your accent icing, specify when this must be received by. If the bride wishes to approve your colour matched icing, agree on a date this must be signed off by.

> I have an order form for a wedding cake which the customer signs. It just says that the design is final and there may be a cost incurred for any changes. I had a bride who changed the design 4 times so I learnt from that! They also pay a 25% deposit at the time of booking as that allows me to buy bits so I'm not out of pocket.
>
> **Kathryn Carter,
> The Kooky Cake Company**

Deposits

Deposits are due when the customer confirms their order and signs and returns the Order Form together with the Terms & Conditions. Taking a deposit ensures you are not out of pocket on the cost of ingredients or time spent should a customer cancel, and also allows you to block out the day they have booked so that you may plan other orders and your work schedule around the order.

For wedding cake orders a deposit of 50% is usual, 25% for other celebration cakes. Short-notice orders should be paid in full at time of order.

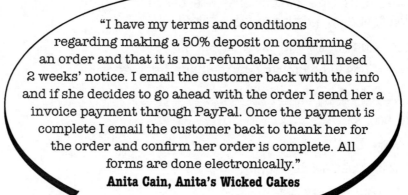

"I have my terms and conditions regarding making a 50% deposit on confirming an order and that it is non-refundable and will need 2 weeks' notice. I email the customer back with the info and if she decides to go ahead with the order I send her a invoice payment through PayPal. Once the payment is complete I email the customer back to thank her for the order and confirm her order is complete. All forms are done electronically."
Anita Cain, Anita's Wicked Cakes

Terms & Conditions

Attached to your Order Form on a separate sheet will be your detailed Terms & Conditions. These form the legal contract between yourself and the customer and are there both to protect you and to ensure that both parties are clear on what to expect. Taking the time to go through these will help avoid any misunderstandings as things progress.

The T&C Template at the end of this chapter should provide you with a starting point/guidelines for your Terms and Conditions which you can then adapt to suit.

Terms & Conditions to include details regarding:

- Price
- Payment methods
- Changes to orders
- Collection
- Cancellations & Refunds
- Allergies

- Deposits
- Payment Dates
- Cake components
- Delivery and set-up
- Portion Guides

"Early on I did have someone cancel an order with very little notice because another family member had ordered a cake elsewhere. I hadn't started to bake, but I had made some preparations and purchased the ingredients. I explained this to the customer who just didn't see my point of view at all, and disputed the notice period. The arrangement back then was cash on delivery and as such I lost out. From that point on, I made it a policy to ensure full payment clears at least a week in advance of the booking. Lesson learnt!"

Melissa Rayner, Fairy Dust Bakery

Hire Agreement

When hiring out things like cake stands or cupcake towers, it's important to be clear on what happens in the event that these are not returned to you. A deposit equal to the total replacement cost should be taken, and refunded once the items have been returned safely. In addition to the deposit there should also be a hire charge, and both of these costs should be outlined clearly on the Order Form and Hire Agreement.

It's always a good idea to mark your stands with your company and contact details. In the event that your stands go missing at a busy venue, staff who come across your stands after the event will be able to contact you directly.

Delivery/Set-Up Details

Because the customer i.e. the Bride, will not be contactable on the day you deliver her cake, it's important that you have absolutely all the information required to make a safe delivery to the venue, plus precise details of where and how the cake will be displayed.

As well as the venue details and contact numbers, details should include your contact person on the day (wedding planner, event manager), how to access the correct part of the venue for delivery, parking and load-in information and exact location of the function room you will be delivering to.

If the bride is having fresh flowers supplied that need to be displayed on the cake, make sure you have the florist details, and a few days prior to the wedding, make contact with both the florist, the venue contact and the wedding planner to ensure everyone is aware of timings. Always allow tons of extra time to reach a venue as traffic and parking at the venue can be unpredictable and being late is simply not an option!

Portion/Cutting Guide

Because the customer, or the venue catering staff, will be cutting your cake it is vital that they understand exactly what size a serving is supposed to be and how to cut it correctly. This seems obvious but people who are not trained to cut a cake tend to cut slices too large and a 100 serving cake quickly becomes a 75 serving one. A tipsy mother of the bride cutting pie size wedding cake slices and later complaining that the cake supplied isn't big enough is quite a common occurrence.

It can be even more disastrous if too large slices are cut from a child's birthday cake and some children are left without cake. The best way to avoid being blamed for other people's cake cutting mistakes is to provide your customers with cake cutting instructions.

Cake company *Wilton* also have some handy guides to print off here
http://www.wilton.com/cakes/cake-cutting-guides/

Important Cake and Allergy information

In addition to the *'Portion Cutting Guide'*, you should supply an *'Important Information'* sheet with each cake. This will outline any safety information relating to your cake, i.e Inedible decorative items, allergens and additives, and choking hazards (edible gems etc). Prior to the event this should be signed and returned by the customer—the responsibility is now on them to ensure that anyone other than them cutting the cake is aware of these details. You should also deliver a copy of this (signed) form with the cake too.

Cake-tastrophes!

If you've ever watched any of the great cake shows on TV (I personally am addicted to *'Ace Of Cakes'*!) you will know that all professional cake makers carry an emergency kit with them, ready to deal with any disasters that arise between their bakery and the venue. Having the right tools, fondant and spare decorations (always make extra flowers etc) with you could mean the difference between a '*cake-tastrophe*' and a '*cake-tastic*' result!

Always be prepared!

We once had a lady who had a three tier white chocolate creation with hand moulded fans and roses. She came to collect it and put it in the back of her car. It was a hot day. She parked illegally while she went off to do some last minute shopping and the car was lifted and taken away. During the lifting process the cake had slipped and the tiers had come apart. She came back with it a couple of hours later and said: "Oh my god! Look what's happened to my cake." And it was just a big mush in the back of the car. All our cakes are baked fresh for our clients, but luckily we carry a stock of cakes in the freezer for last minute orders. We pulled several from the freezer, and had 5 people working on recreating this wedding cake for her. So thankfully we managed to turn it around for her.'
Mich Turner, Little Venice Cake Company

Claire's Cupcakes

123 Vanilla Rd, Yumsville, YM 123
info@clairescakes.com
(212) 123 4567

Cake Order Form

Date Required	
Type of Event	
Date order placed	
Customer Name	
Email	
Address	
Phone (Home and Mobile)	
Emergency contact	
Collection day and time OR Delivery venue and time	
Contact name and no. at venue	
Service venue / time of service	
Name of design (if any)	
Portions Required? No. of tiers and sizes / No. of mini cakes	
Stacked / pillars / separators?	
Stand Hire Required?	
Colors—swatch to be sent?	
Modelled figures?	
Flowers? Fresh, Silk, Sugar	

	Size	Flavor	Filling	Covering	Marzipan	Design notes
Tier One						
Tier Two						
Tier Three						
Tier Four						
Cutting Cake						

	Theme (if any)	Colors	Age on cake	Candles added	Inscription (NB spellings)	
Birthday Cakes						
Cost of cake						
Delivery / setup charge						
Hire of stand, knife etc						
Security Deposit for Stand						
TOTAL PRICE						
Deposit Paid						
Date Deposit Paid						
Balance Due:						
Balance Due by						

Your cake is very important to us. Please take the time to check your copy of the order form carefully and let us know immediately if there are any mistakes or if changes are needed.
"I agree to the Terms & Conditions attached to this contract and agree that I am the person responsible for all payments and decisions regarding this cake order."

Customer Signature: Date:

Claire's Cupcakes

123 Vanilla Rd, Yumsville, YM 123
info@clairescakes.com

(212) 123 4567

Terms & Conditions Of Sale

Prices
You agree to pay the company the price as quoted on your signed Order Form.

Bookings & Deposits
All Orders and Booking Dates are only secured with a non-refundable deposit. Once deposits are received and cleared your booking date will then be fully secured. All Wedding Cake orders require a non-refundable deposit of 50%. Other celebration cakes require a non-refundable deposit of 25%.

Final Payments
Full Balance is due 4 weeks prior to the cake delivery date as specified on your order form. On your initial invoice the date of the full balance will be included and a reminder of the final amount will be emailed to you no less than 7 days before payment is due. Failure to make payment of the remanding balance may result in your order being cancelled and your date being made available to someone else.

Payment methods accepted are Cash or Credit Card.

Late or Non-Payments
Late or non-payments could result in loss of your booking date. In the event of a late or non-payment, the order will not proceed until alternative funding has been agreed and payment made in full. In these circumstances, subsequent completion of the order on the required date will not be guaranteed and becomes Subject To Availability.

Cancellations
Wedding Cakes: 12 weeks or more: 50% of the total cost will be retained. Less than 12 weeks: 100% of total cost payable.

Other Celebration Cakes: 4 weeks or more: 25% non-refundable deposit will be retained. Less than 4 weeks: 100% of total cost payable.

All Cancellations must be made in writing. Verbal phone cancellations will not be binding.

Change of Wedding Date
If, for any reason you wish to re-arrange the date of your wedding, we will try its best to accommodate these changes without any additional charges provided sufficient notice is given and that we are able to provide a cake for the re-arranged wedding date. However, if we are fully booked on your new wedding date and cannot provide the wedding cake, it will not be possible to refund your deposit. The limiting factor with any cake provision is usually the cake set-up. As a compromise, it may be possible to provide you with a cake prior to your wedding

date, but under these circumstances it will become your responsibility to collect, deliver and set-up the cake at the venue. If you cancel your wedding cake order with us after requesting a change of date no refunds will be made to you (the client) under any circumstances.

Stand Hire

We have a wide range of stands, bases and cupcake tower stands available for hire. All stands require a deposit, in addition to the hire charges, which is fully refundable on return of the hired stand. Any damages will be deducted from the deposit. In the event that damages are excessive, or a loss has occurred then the deposit will be retained.

Delivery/Collection

On the day of collection, your order may be collected at a pre-arranged time, as agreed on your Order Form. Should you wish to change the collection details we will do our best to accommodate, but cannot guaranteed availability.
Deliveries: We will deliver at the time and address agreed with the customer on the invoice. If we can't deliver because there is no one to receive the product or the address provided is wrong, the product will return to our bakery and will be held for a maximum time of 24 hours.

Delivery/Setting Up of Your Cake At Venues

Cakes should be inspected on receipt to ensure that they were not damaged in transit, as you (or any third party taking delivery, e.g. hotel/wedding planner etc.) shall be solely responsible for any damage to any products which occurs (i) after the delivery or collection of any product and/or (ii) as a result of failure to follow any instructions/advice we may give in respect of storage or setting up or of further transportation of the cake.

Allergies

Any special recipe request such as 'no nuts' will be met wherever possible. However, whilst your chosen cake will not be made with nuts or a nut product, no absolute nut free guarantees can be given, as some ingredients are not guaranteed nut free by the manufacturers. Allergy information will be provided with all orders.

I Have Read and Accept the Above Terms & Conditions

Signed: **Print Name:**

Date:

Claire's Cupcakes

123 Vanilla Rd, Yumsville, YM 123
info@clairescakes.com

(212) 123 4567

Invoice

Invoice To: Date:

Customer reference:

Invoice Number:

Order Date:

Details:

Order Total:

Amount Received:

Payment Amount Due:

Balance Outstanding:

Balance Due Date:

Claire's Cupcakes

Delivery/Cake Set-Up

Delivery To:	Date:
Name of Contact at Venue:	Customer Name:
Contact Mobile Number:	Delivery Time/
Venue Details/Address:	Set-Up Start Time:
Name Of Function Room:	Cake To Be Set-up by:

Notes Re: Venue/Access/Parking:

Delivery Of Cake/OR Set-Up Of Cake? (Delete as appropriate)

Details:

Equipment Supplied (Deposit Held):

Order Total:

Amount Received:

Cake and Important Information Received In Good Condition :

Signature:
Date and Time:

Print Name:

Comments:

Cakes should be inspected on receipt to ensure that they were not damaged in transit, as you (as named above) shall be solely responsible for any damage to any products which occurs (i) after the delivery or collection of any product and/or (ii) as a result of failure to follow any instructions/advice we may give in respect of storage or setting up or of further transportation of the cake.

Claire's Cupcakes

123 Vanilla Rd, Yumsville, YM 123
info@clairescakes.com
(212) 123 4567

Important Information

To: Date:

                                        Customer name:

Important information regarding your cake is given below. We require you to sign and acknowledge this prior to release of the order. You also hereby agree to pass this information on to any involved parties.

The following items on this cake are ***NOT*** edible and must be removed before cake is consumed:

Allergy information

Your cake has been prepared in a kitchen where some allergens may be present, and therefore we cannot guarantee the cake will not contain any traces of the following:

• Nuts
• Peanuts
• Sesame seeds
• Seafood/shellfish
• Milk/eggs/dairy
• Gluten

Cutting Guide

In order to ensure your cake produces the required amount of servings for your even, we have attached a cutting guide. Please ensure any staff cutting this cake has a copy of this.

Customer Signature: Print Name:

Date and Time:

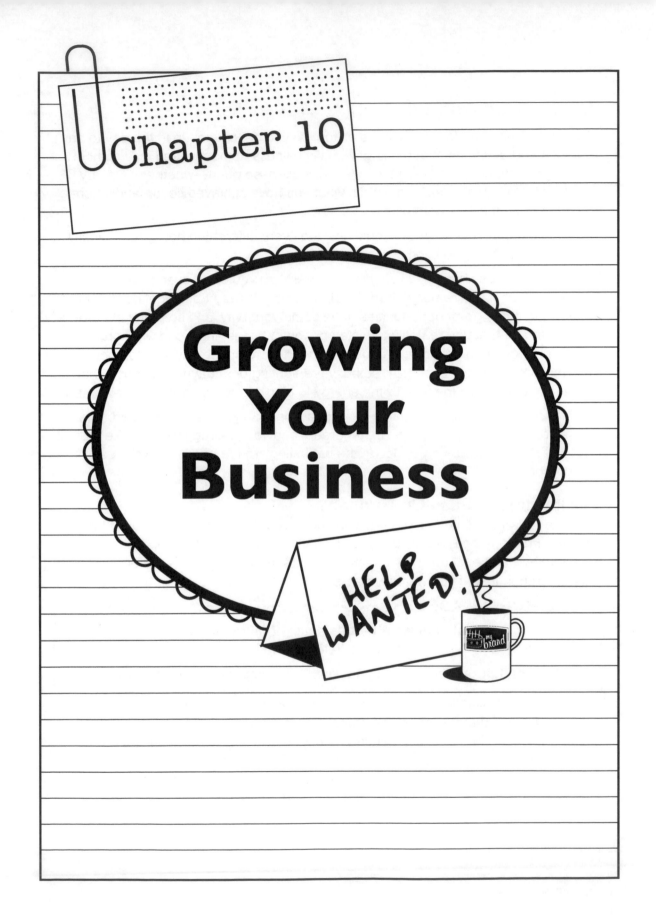

Chapter 10

Growing Your Business

HELP WANTED!

Review and Reflect

When you're self-employed, it can be all too easy to get caught up in the day to day demands and deadlines that running a small business demands, and lose sight of your original goals. It's important to take stock every so often—whether it's every 6 months or every year—and think about what you have achieved so far, and where you hope to take things from here.

You may find that your business could now look very different to how you originally imagined. Is that a good thing or a bad thing?

Maybe the business has grown so much quicker than you could even have dreamed, and you feel as if you're being dragged along on a runaway train, fighting to stay in control? So many great opportunities have come your way, and so many big orders are flooding in, that you're battling to stay on top of things and wondering how on earth you're going to continue to cope. You need more space, more help, more time, more knowledge, but you're so busy fire-fighting on a day-to-day basis that you simply don't have the time or the energy to plan the next phase of development.

Or perhaps things have been much more of a slog than you had anticipated. The orders you hoped for just haven't materialised, and you're struggling to make a profit and retain the enthusiasm you had in the beginning. You're not sure if you really want to continue.

Call It Quits, or Push On Through?

Whatever challenges you are currently facing in your business, rest assured that for every problem there is a solution, and what you are currently going through has been experienced by thousands of entrepreneurs, and cake bakers, before you. You will get through this. If you want to, that is.

> **Most importantly—business situation aside—**
> **how are *YOU* feeling?**
>
> **Are you happy? Is running your own business what you expected?**

Are you enjoying the majority of the process, or have you come to dread each day? Turning a hobby into a career can be hugely challenging, and there's no shame in admitting that actually, this may not be for you after all. Yes, you may feel embarrassed admitting to all the friends and family who have so eagerly supported you that, actually, this just isn't working out for you.

Before you walk away, let's troubleshoot and look at some of the most common reasons for Cake Business Fatigue. What changes need to occur for you to have more fun and make more money, and what steps do you need to take to implement these changes?

Problem	Possible Solution
Loneliness: you miss the day-to-day interaction with other people	Hire some shared space in a commercial kitchen, or hire some part-time help at home. Join some local women's business networking groups.
Running out of space at home	Look for an affordable shared kitchen space. Could you convert a garage or improve the space at home?
Bored of making large amounts of the same things i.e cupcakes	Consider employing help with the more basic tasks (mixing, baking). You can still retain quality control while delegating simpler tasks.
Large orders and way too many cakes to make	As above, but outsourcing the baking part of production completely. You could start off employing local moms to bake from home. Or if you have space, part-timers who come to you.
Bogged down with day to day admin tasks.	Hire a bookkeeper, virtual PA or part time help to assist you with invoicing, packing and shipping goods, delivering cakes etc.
You don't enjoy selling, but need to find more stockists for your cakes/cookies.	Find a part-time "sales rep": an outgoing friend who will visit stores and cafes to get orders for you. Pay them on commission to incentivise them.
Not enough orders	Could the quality of your cakes be improved upon? Or do you need to revisit the Marketing and PR tasks?

Problem	Possible Solution
Plenty of orders, not enough profit	Are you charging enough? Do you need to reduce your outgoings and costs?
You're working way too many hours a day and have lost all sense of work/life balance	Read on to the end of this Chapter, and consider all of the above options so that you're working Smarter, not Harder!

If Working From Home Just Isn't Working Any More!

When your kitchen cupboards, spare room or garage is bursting at the seams, and your business seems to have taken over every aspect of your life, physically and mentally, it's so tempting to dream of hiring a space dedicated to your business. Moving from home to your own kitchen or store is a huge leap and it's important to get the timing right.

Lack of space

Unlike many other home workers who can get by with a laptop, some files, and a small office area in the corner of a room, running a cake business obviously involves a lot of STUFF! And the sheer amount of stuff can quickly grow, to the point where you're tripping over packaging in the hallway, stacking supplies in the bedroom and hogging the dining table with your makeshift production lines.

Can you afford to hire space?

The great thing about working from home is that it's pretty much free. When a business is starting out, it's vital to keep your overheads low. So while you would love a nice, spacious commercial kitchen, can you really afford it and do you want the worry of having to pay the rent each month?

Will you miss the convenience?

As you take that leisurely stroll from the kitchen to your home office, or pop some laundry in the dryer while you wait for a cake to bake, think about what you may miss if you no longer worked from home. Yes, you're excited about separating work and home life, and desperate for your home to return to being just a home, but sometimes the grass is always greener. Getting business premises means commuting, being away from the house all day every day, and losing all the perks that home working can offer. Are you ready for that?

It's Lonely at the Top (And the Bottom, and Middle!)

One of those pitfalls of working for yourself can be the isolation factor, also known as Cabin Fever! Working at home, alone, isolated from the world, in the same place can slowly but surely drive a person round the bend. Impossible as it may sound, you might even find yourself starting to miss those annoying colleagues and that irritating boss!

It's easy to assume that hiring a kitchen space will provide the solution to the problem—but the money spent on rent could be used to hire extra help…which would provide an extra pair of hands AND the company you are missing. Otherwise you may find yourself working alone in a lovely kitchen space, and feeling just as isolated!

Fortunately, there are some things you can do if you feel isolated and a little bit lonely. One of those things is to make sure you leave the house every day, regardless of how busy you feel, or how cold, wet or windy it may be outside!

Even though the majority of cake business work requires you to be in your kitchen, you could set aside a certain time each afternoon for answering and sending emails, calling back customers or keeping on top of your blog and social networking. And that can be done from just about anywhere, if you have a laptop. Take a walk in the fresh air to your favourite café, pitch up for even half an hour to an hour to do your online work whilst enjoying a well-earned latte, then stroll home again— even just an hour away from the kitchen can give you that boost you need to get through the rest of the day and stop you from going stir crazy! Something as simple as going for a walk just to get a breath of fresh air can take away that sensation of the walls closing in around you.

Move, or Improve?

If you've considered all of the above, but feel that it's really time to move on and move out, consider the following:

- Is the company earning enough to pay rent? How much can you afford?

- Don't run before you can walk—you may be on a high from a couple of big orders and feel the time has come to trade up. Can you be 100% sure that the business will continue at this rate?

- Are you able to make a long-term commitment (you may need to sign a lease anywhere from 12-48 months)

- Are you happy to share a kitchen space, or do you require a place of your own?

Finding a Kitchen Outside The Home

When looking for a kitchen space away from home, there are a few options.

Local cafes, restaurants, church or community halls

Often premises like this will have a fully working kitchen which has already been approved by the state, but it may not be in use all day every day. Perhaps a local restaurant only opens for evening meals. Their chef starts work at 2pm each day to prep for the evening, meaning they may consider allowing you to use the kitchen from 9am–1.30pm.

Or a local church hall has a large kitchen that is used mainly on weekends, and the odd coffee morning. Perhaps you could be using this during the week? These kinds of businesses may be open to making some extra money by renting the space to you during their down time—and it could be a situation that works well for both parties!

And the bonus is that an existing commercial kitchen should already be certified AND have most of the cooking equipment you need in place.

You will also need to consider things like storage of your ingredients and refrigeration (if appropriate), Will there be a secure space or cupboard where you can store and leave all your ingredients and tools? Or will you have to bring these with you every day (not ideal!)

Make a list of all the things you need—counter space, oven capacity, food mixer, cooling rack, baking pans. Are you allowed to bring in some of your own equipment? Where will it be stored?

Can you use the kitchen at the hours that suit you? What about getting in and locking up—will you have your own keys? Is it in a safe area if you are working there alone? Will you always be assured of a parking space?

All these factors should be taken into consideration before making a commitment. Once you've discussed all this thoroughly with the owner or pastor and agreed on terms and a price, it's really important to put all this in writing—see the Sublet Agreement template later in this chapter. Your business will now depend on your ability to use this kitchen, so you need to be clear on notice periods and your responsibilities, and the owner needs to formalize exactly what they are allowing you to do and when. A written agreement like this will protect both parties.

If the kitchen owner is hesitant to put things in writing, be wary. While informal agreements can often work fine, often misunderstandings can arise—especially where money is concerned—so putting everything that you have verbally agreed in writing should be a simple way to let everyone know where they stand.

Hiring Your Own Commercial Kitchen

You could look for a dedicated commercial kitchen space that will be solely for your business, and this will mean being completely responsible for the lease and premises—a big commitment. Or you could start by looking for shared commercial space—perhaps another food company already has great premises but are not working at full capacity and have space to sublet an area to a small company like yourself. Many cities now have incubator kitchens, created with small start-up food companies in mind. These can be a great way to share space with like-minded people too!

Open a Cake Shop or Café

Many cake bakers dream of having their own beautiful cake storefront—a place to chat to customers, be part of the local community and show off their amazing range of cakes and bakes. Opening a retail premises is a whole different ballgame to running a business from home. It will require a significant up-front financial investment, plus you'll be responsible for large overheads for staff and rent each month. Are you ready for that sort of commitment? Staff costs are high, so it's likely that you will need to work there every single day, and often have to stay on once the store is closed to finish cake orders. Taking holidays will be tricky, and the business will become the absolute focus of your life. Is this really what you dreamed of? There's a lot to consider before taking such a big leap!

"Try to look at any premises offering rent free periods—as so many shops are empty in my town there were one or two options that offered this (although I did not go for one of them in the end). Make sure you get a contractor (or two) in to look at property to quote you for any work needed. Try to get as short a lease as possible whilst still looking at best rent costs, and ask for a break clause—this allows you to get out of the lease at an earlier point.

Location is key—try to visit the area at different times of the day/week to assess the passing trade. Look at car parking options for your customers too.

I spoke to my contractor and asked for timescales then added a few weeks on to allow for any problems before I committed to an opening date. Having premises is totally different to doing cake making as a business from home—you have to stick to your advertised opening hours so there are various cons linked to that like sickness/holiday cover, childcare issues. I work longer hours now than I ever have and find my biggest worry would be becoming ill and letting customers down.

Karen Bill, Designa Cake & Cupcake Café

Claire's Cupcakes

123 Vanilla Rd, Yumsville, YM 123
info@clairescakes.com
(212) 123 4567

Use Of Kitchen Agreement

Date:

This agreement between **Claire Cake** and **James Owner** is for the use of the kitchen located at: **Le Gourmand Locale, Vanilla Lane, Yumsville, YM 123**.

This kitchen is currently registered with Yumsville County Health Dept. and James Owner confirms the premises has fully complied with all required codes.

Use of the premises by Claire Cake includes use of the Kitchen, Production Areas and the following equipment:

- Sinks with hot and cold running water
- Use of 2 x industrial ovens and hob/burners
- Two large work areas/countertops
- Cooling racks, cake pans, large pots, knives and any miscellaneous kitchen utensils
- Refrigeration During Production Time Only
- Use of one 5 shelf storage pantry with lock

All work surfaces, utensils and baking pans to be cleaned and returned to storage prior to end of shift. Both parties agree to maintain cleanliness in accordance with state guidelines.

Any issues regarding to cleanliness or tidiness of kitchen to be reported to the other party, in writing, within 24 hours of issue arising.

Days and Hours Agreed: Monday–Friday: 9am–1.30pm. Saturdays: 4am–9am.
Locked storage area with 24 hour access. Claire Cake to be allocated set of keys and alarm code to allow access. Parking: Allocated parking spot to the rear of premises, close to access door, available during these times, but cannot be guaranteed outwith these due to staff requirements.

Rental Amount: $300 per calendar month, plus 2 large (8 serving) chocolate fudge cakes—to be sold in restaurant—per week (delivered each Monday and Thursday no later than 1.30pm). Rent payable in advance on the 1st of each month. Rent includes use of kitchen, equipment, utilities and repairs.

Length Of Contract: Until further notice. During 3 month trial period, either party can end lease giving 14 days notice. Thereafter thirty (30) days written notice required from either party.

Owner:	Tenant:	Witnessed by:
Name:	Name:	Name:
Address:	Address:	Address:
Signature:	Signature:	Signature:
Date:	Date:	Date:

Growing Your Business

Get Help
If you're in the fortunate position to have enough orders coming in that you're already working at full capacity, it's time to get help. You need to be working *SMARTER*, not *HARDER*!

Think about what you could delegate to others. Could someone come to your house/kitchen to take over some of the baking tasks so that you could spend that time decorating or on admin? If you hate selling, could an outgoing friend act as your "sales rep" and go out and get orders from local shops, offices and cafes? If you hate admin, could someone oversee your invoices and book-keeping? Not that computer savvy? Rope in a teenager to manage your Facebook page and update the photos on your website.

With the right help you could double your output without increasing your actual working hours—now that's smart!

Expand Your Products
When you've worked hard to gain customers, and you'd like to expand your business, it makes sense to think what else you could be selling to the same people. If local cafes are already buying your large cakes to sell by the slice, could you also sell them cookies, muffins or even pastries or tarts? In the winter they may welcome apple pies? If your wedding and birthday cakes are going down a storm, could you also set up a party catering side to the business? This will depend on your skills, the direction you want your business to go in, and your customers. But by adding to your product ranges, you could be selling more products, to more people.

Sell to Shops and Cafes
If your main business is in wedding cakes, you will likely find yourself with a lot of down time during the winter months. If you haven't already considered this, what about supplying to local stores, cafes, coffee shops etc. This can provide a good source of year-round trade.

Offices and Local Business
Unless you live in a very rural area, there are bound to be a wide range of local businesses within a 5-10 mile radius of your home. Perhaps you could approach a few of the larger ones about visiting their office one afternoon a week to sell your cakes and cookies—perhaps suggest a "*Cake Friday*". This would be a nice treat for

their workers and a good income source for you. If you time it right you could fit in several businesses per afternoon and make some decent money. Some big businesses are keen to find low-cost ways to increase staff morale—perhaps the company could pay you for a set number of cakes each week or once a month for their staff. This means one drop-off and one large payment, much easier than selling by the slice to each individual. Imagine if you had a few large orders like this each week—it could seriously help your income.

Run Classes

Are you good with people? Do you like the idea of passing on your skills and meeting lots of new people? Running classes could be ideal for you. Cupcake decorating classes are huge right now and can be a great way to add to your income. Depending on your skill level you may feel able to run a variety of classes, from basic cake decorating through to more specialist sugar paste and fondant flower classes etc. Have a look and see what else is on offer in your local area, and consider whether you have the space at home, or would need to hire a venue. Maybe even go on a course elsewhere to see how they run the day and what's included. Do your research and decide if running courses is right for you and your business.

> "I am busy setting up a new side to the business—The Kooky Bakery. I am having 2 vans out delivering fresh sandwiches and cakes on a daily basis. Everything on the vans will be home made by hand. It's very exciting!"
>
> **Kathryn Carter,**
> **The Kooky Cake Company**

Work/Life Balance

Now that your business is growing, it's quite likely that you'll readily admit that it seems to have taken over your life. When you're passionate about what you do, you'll happily spend every waking moment working towards your dreams. But it's impossible to keep the adrenaline and crazy working hours of those first few years going in the long term. Not only will you burn out, but your personal life will suffer, and no amount of business success is worth losing your health, friends or family for. It's time to review how you work, and look at any changes that could be made now to help you move forward in a healthier and happier way.

We all need days just to dream, create and kick back—but finding "*me time*" can sometimes seem impossible when you have a hundred tasks to juggle. It's important to step back and look at how you structure your days and see if there is a way you can make improvements.

Have a think about when you work best, what tasks you have each day, and how you may be able to structure your working day to maximize your time. Perhaps you like to bake in the mornings, as it's a relatively mindless task that allows you to ease into the day. Then after lunch you feel more revved up and able to tackle things like emails, PR and marketing and calling customers. Great, structure your day around that.

Don't forget to factor in time for lunch and a stroll. I've also included a section for 'Personal tasks' as you may have children to factor into your day, or other commitments outside the business that you need to work around. Once you've completed this, pin it somewhere you will see every day and feel free to adapt and tweak your schedule until you find one that works for you!

The Icing On The Cake

Whatever you decide for your business, the future is in your hands. Everything you achieve will be because of your effort, your hard work, your passion and your blood, sweat and tears. Whatever you dream of for your business is entirely possible, and *YOU* can make it happen.

Creating a fun, rewarding business is one of the best gifts you can ever give yourself, and to be able to spend your days doing something you truly love is a dream that can absolutely become a reality.

Don't forget to take time to stop, smell the roses (or the cookies!) and give yourself a big pat on the back for coming this far.

I wish you the very best of luck in all that you do. Here's to the future and all that it holds for you! *Good Luck! And don't forget to HAVE FUN!*

Your Working Day		
	Personal Tasks	Work tasks
8am		
9		
10		
11		
12		
1pm		
2		
3		
4		
5		
6		
Evenings		

Resources

Blog Building Tools

Wordpress	www.wordpress.org
Typepad	www.typepad.com
Blogger	www.blogger.com

Business Help

SCORE: Service Corps of Retired Executives	www.score.org
SBDC: Small Business Development Center	www.sba.gov

Business Plan Templates

SCORE: Service Corps of Retired Executives	www.score.org/template_gallery.html
SBA: Small Business Administration	www.sba.gov/starting_business/planning/writingplan.html
WBDC: Women's Business Development Center	www.wbdc.org

Cake Forums and Inspiration

Bakerella	www.bakerella.com
Cake Central	www.cakecentral.com
Cake Journal	www.cakejournal.com
Cake Spy	www.cakespy.com
The Cake Lab	www.thecakelab.com
Cake Wrecks	www.cakewrecks.com
Edible Artists Network	www.edibleartistsnetwork.com
Fans Of Cake Baker	www.facebook.com/fansofcakebaker
Wilton Cake Cutting Guides	www.wilton.com/cakes/cake-cutting-guides

Car Advertising

Car Wraps	www.vehiclewrapsusa.com
Custom Car Sun Shades	www.epromos.com/customized-car-sun-shades/_/N-11039

Company Names Registers and Trademarks

US Secretary Of State	www.secstates.com
US Copyright Office	www.copyright.gov
US Patents & Trademarks Office	www.uspto.gov

Domain Names
GoDaddy — www.godaddy.com
Register — www.register.com
NameScure — www.namesecure.com

Education
Cake Central — www.cakecentral.com/classes
Wilton — www.wilton.com

Image Gallery Sites
Shrink Pictures — www.shrinkpictures.com
Flickr — http://flickr-gallery.com
Pinterest — http://pinterest.com

Online Store Building Sites
Shopify — www.shopify.com
Big Cartel — www.bigcartel.com
Ekm Powershop — www.ekmpowershop.com
Moonfruit — www.moonfruit.com
Volusion — www.volusion.com

Payment Processing
Paypal — www.paypal.com
Square — https://squareup.com/

Printing
E Print — www.eprintfast.com
Printing Center USA — www.printingcenterusa.com
USA Printing Trade — www.usaprintingtrade.com

Suppliers
BRP Box Shop — www.brpboxshop.com
Bakers Kitchen — www.thebakerskitchen.net
Cake Stands, Asymmetrical — www.cakestands.com
CK Products — www.ckproducts.com/
Koyal, Cake Boxes — www.koyalwholesale.com
Global Sugar Art — www.globalsugarart.com
Sugarcraft — www.sugarcraft.com
US Cake Supply — www.uscakesupply.com
Wilton — www.wilton.com

State Home-Based Kitchen Guidelines and Business Resources

The rules and guidelines for operating a food business vary from state to state, so it's important to consult with the various departments at a local level to ensure you are following the correct procedures for your business.

Alabama

State Website	alabama.gov
Information on Starting a Business	alabama.gov/portal/secondary.jsp?page=Business
Department of Public Health 334-206-5375	adph.org
Business License: at county level:	ador.state.al.us/licenses/index.html
Business Structure Filing	sos.state.al.us/BusinessServices/Default.aspx
Business Name Registration	sos.state.al.us/BusinessServices/Default.aspx
Department of Revenue	ador.state.al.us/bus.html
Small Business Administration Office	sba.gov/localresources/district/al/index.html

Alaska

State Website	Alaska.gov
Health code and permits	Contact your city or county health dept
Submit plan for approval	dec.state.ak.us/eh/fss/Food/Opening.html
Business License	commerce.state.ak.us/CBP/
Business Structure Filing	commerce.state.ak.us/occ/cforms.htm
Business Name Registration	commerce.state.ak.us/occ/register.html
Business Tax Registration	tax.alaska.gov
Resources for Starting a Business	alaska.gov/businessHome.html
Small Business Administration Office	sba.gov/localresources/district/ak/index.html

Arizona

State Website	az.gov
Food Safety and Environmental Services	azdhs.gov/phs/oeh/fses/
Health inspections handled at county level.	
Business Structure Filing	azcc.gov/divisions/corporations/filings/forms/index.htm
Business Tax Registration	aztaxes.gov
Information on Starting a Business	azcommerce.com/BusAsst/SmallBiz/
Small Business Administration Office	sba.gov/localresources/district/ar/index.html

Arkansas

State Website	portal.arkansas.gov
Business Structure Filing	sos.arkansas.gov/corp_ucc_business.html
Business Name Registration	sos.arkansas.gov/corp_ucc_business.html
Business Tax Registration	dfa.arkansas.gov/offices/incomeTax/Pages/default.aspx
Arkansas Small Business Development Center	asbdc.ualr.edu/
Small Business Administration Office	sba.gov/localresources/district/ar/index.html

California

State Website	ca.gov
Business Structure Filing	sos.ca.gov/business/be/forms.htm
Business Name Registration	Contact your County Recorder Clerk's Office
Business Tax Registration	taxes.ca.gov
Information on Starting a Business in California	calbusiness.ca.gov
Small Business Administration Office	sba.gov/localresources/district/ca/

Colorado

State Website	colorado.gov
State Public Health Dept.	cdphe.state.co.us/regulations/consumer/
Business Structure Filing	sos.state.co.us/pubs/business/main.htm
Business Name Registration	sos.state.co.us/biz/FileDoc.do
Business Tax Registration	colorado.gov/revenue/tax
City or County Business Licenses	Contact your local tax department
Information on Starting a Business	colorado.gov
Small BusinessAdministration Office index.html	sba.gov/localresources/district/co/

Connecticut

State Website	ct.gov
Business license registration	Contact your local town clerk
Business Name Registration	ct.gov/sots/site/default.asp
Health code and permits	Contact your city or county health dept.
City or county Business Licenses	Contact your city or county health dept.
Small Business Administration Office	sba.gov/localresources/district/ct/index.html

DC

State Website	dc.gov
Health Code Requirements and Permit	dchealth.dc.gov

Business Structure Filing	dcra.dc.gov/DC/DCRA/
Business Name Registration	dcra.dc.gov/DC/DCRA/
Business Tax Registration	taxpayerservicecenter.com/fr500/
Information on Starting a Business	brc.dc.gov
Small Business Administration Office	sba.gov/localresources/district/dc/index.html

Delaware

State Website	delaware.gov
Department of Agriculture	dda.delaware.gov/
Business Structure Filing	corp.delaware.gov/howtoform.shtml
Business Name Registration	sos.delaware.gov/
Business Tax Registration	onestop.delaware.gov/osbrlpublic/Home.jsp
Information on Starting a Business	dedo.delaware.gov
Small Business Administration Office	sba.gov/localresources/district/de/index.html

Florida

State Website	myflorida.com
Business Licenses, Permits and Regulation	myflorida.com/taxonomy/business/
Business Structure Filing	sunbiz.org
Business Name Registration	efile.sunbiz.org/ficregintro.html
Business Tax Registration	dor.myflorida.com/dor/taxes/registration.html
Information on Starting a Business	myflorida.com/taxonomy/business/
Small Business Administration Office	sba.gov/localresources/district/fl/

Georgia

State Website	georgia.gov
Environmental Health Food Service	health.state.ga.us/programs/envservices/foodservice.asp
Business Structure Filing	sos.georgia.gov/corporations/
Business Name Registration	sos.ga.gov/firststop/faqs.htm
Business Tax Registration	etax.dor.ga.gov/ctr/formsreg.aspx
Small Business Administration Office	sba.gov/localresources/district/ga/index.html

Hawaii

State Website	hawaii.gov
Health code and permits	Contact your city or county health dept.
City or county Business Licenses	Contact your city or county health dept.
Business Structure Filing	ehawaii.gov

Business Name Registration   hbe.ehawaii.gov/BizEx/home.eb
Business Tax Registration   hbe.ehawaii.gov/BizEx/home.eb
Information on Starting a new Business   hawaii.gov/dbedt/business/start_grow/
Small Business Administration Office   sba.gov/localresources/district/hi/index.html

Idaho

State Website   idaho.gov
Health code and permits   Contact your city or county health dept.
Licence applications   cdhd.idaho.gov/pdfs/food/food_estab_license_app.pdf

Facility requirements   tinyurl.com/idahobakery
Business Structure Filing   sos.idaho.gov/corp/corindex.htm
Business Name Registration   sos.idaho.gov/corp/ABNform.htm
Business Tax Registration   labor.idaho.gov/applications/ibrs/ibr.aspx
Information on Starting a new Business   business.idaho.gov
Small Business Administration Office   sba.gov/localresources/district/id/index.html

Illinois

State Website   illinois.gov
Health code and permits   Contact your city or county health dept.
City or county Business Licenses   Contact your city or county health dept.
Business Structure Filing   business.illinois.gov/registration.cfm
Business Name Registration   cyberdriveillinois.com/
Business Tax Registration   business.illinois.gov/registration.cfm
Small Business Administration Office   sba.gov/localresources/district/il/index.html

Indiana

State Website   in.gov
Department of Health   in.gov/isdh/
Application for food service   in.gov/isdh/files/SF49677_R5-05.pdf
Business Structure Filing   in.gov/sos/business/2381.htm
Business Name Registration   in.gov/sos/business/2436.htm
Business Tax Registration   in.gov/dor/3963.htm
Information on Starting a Business   in.gov/ai/business
Small Business Administration Office   sba.gov/localresources/district/in/index.html

Iowa

State Website   iowa.gov
Rules and regulations   dia.iowa.gov/food/
Business Structure Filing   sos.state.ia.us/business/
Business Name Registration   sos.state.ia.us/business/index.html

Business Tax Registration	idr.iowa.gov/CBA/start.asp
Information on Starting a Business	iowa.gov/Business_and_Economic_ Development
Small Business Administration Office	sba.gov/localresources/district/ia

Kansas

State Website	kansas.gov
Health code and permits	Contact your city or county health dept.
Food Code	kdheks.gov/pdf/regs/28-36.pdf
Business Name Registration	kssos.org/
Business Tax Registration	ksrevenue.org/busregistration.htm
Information on Starting a Business	kssos.org/ fhsu.edu/ksbdc/
Small Business Administration Office	sba.gov/localresources/district/ks

Kentucky

State Website	kentucky.gov
Health code and permits	Contact your city or county health dept.
Business license	revenue.ky.gov/business/register.htm
Business Structure Filing	sos.ky.gov/business/filings/
Business Name Registration	sos.ky.gov/business/filings/
Business Tax Registration	revenue.ky.gov/business/register.htm
Information on Starting a Business	kentucky.gov/business
State Department of Agriculture.	kyagr.com

Louisiana

State Website	louisiana.gov
Health code and permits	Contact your city or county health dept.
City or County Business Licenses	Contact your city or county health dept.
Business Structure Filing	sos.louisiana.gov
Business Name Registration	sos.louisiana.gov
Business Tax Registration	rev.louisiana.gov/sections/business/intro. aspx
Information on Starting a Business	louisiana.gov/Business/Grow_a_Business/
Small Business Administration Office	sba.gov/localresources/district/la/index.html

Maine

State Website	maine.gov
Health code and permits	Contact your city or county health dept.
City or County Business Licenses	Contact your city or county health dept.
Business Structure Filing	maine.gov/sos/cec/corp/
Business Tax Registration	maine.gov/cgi-bin/online/suwtaxreg/index

Information on Starting a Business in Maine   maine.gov/portal/business/starting.html

Small Business Administration Office   sba.gov/localresources/district/me

Maryland

State Website   maryland.gov

Health code and permits   Contact your city or county health dept.

City or County Business Licenses   Contact your city or county health dept.

Business Structure Filing   dat.state.md.us/sdatweb/sdatforms.html#entity

Business Name Registration   dat.state.md.us/sdatweb/nameappl.pdf

Information on Starting a Business in Maryland   tinyurl.com/8avbbp

Small Business Administration Office   sba.gov/about-offices-content/2/3120

Massachusetts

State WebsiteHealth code and permits   Contact your city or county health dept.

City or County Business Licenses   mass.gov/Eeohhs2/docs/dph/environmental/foodsafety/food_app.pdf

Massachusetts Food Business Start Up Guide   tinyurl.com/62mztxu

Information on Starting a Business in MA   tinyurl.com/2rar46

Small Business Administration Office   sba.gov/about-offices-content/2/3162

Massachusetts Department of Agriculture   mass.gov/agr

Michigan

State Website   michigan.gov

Health code and permits   Contact your city or county health dept.

City or County Business Licenses   Contact your city or county health dept.

Dept. of Agriculture   mda-info@michigan.gov

Small Business Administration Office   sba.gov/about-offices-content/2/3121

Business Name Registration   michigan.gov/sos

Minnesota

State Website   state.mn.us

Health code and permits   Contact your city or county health dept.

Starting a Food Business in Minnesota   tinyurl.com/3s7n5ds

Business Structure Filing   sos.state.mn.us/index.aspx?page=92

Business Name Registration   sos.state.mn.us/index.aspx?page=92

Business Tax Registration   mndor.state.mn.us/tp/webreg.html

Information on Starting a Business   tinyurl.com/jjrob

Small Business Administration Office   sba.gov/about-offices-content/2/3121

Mississippi

State Website	mississippi.gov
Health code and permits	Contact your city or county health dept.
State Dept. of Health	msdh.state.ms.us/msdhsite/_static/30,3432,77,311.html
Regulations	msdh.state.ms.us/msdhsite/_static/30,0,77,60.html
Permit application	msdh.state.ms.us/msdhsite/_static/resources/432.pdf
Business Name Registration	sos.ms.gov/business_services.aspx
Business Tax Registration	tax.ms.gov/regist.html
Small Business Administration Office	sba.gov/about-offices-content/2/3125

Missouri

State Website	mo.gov
Health code and permits	Contact your city or county health dept.
Department of Health.	health.mo.gov/safety/foodsafety/faq.php
Missouri food code	health.mo.gov/safety/foodsafety/foodcode.php
Business Structure Filing	sos.mo.gov/business/corporations/startBusiness.asp
Business Name Registration	sos.mo.gov/
Business Tax Registration	dor.mo.gov/business/register/
Information on Starting a Business	ms.gov/ms_sub_template.jsp?Category_ID=3
Small Business Administration Office	sba.gov/about-offices-content/2/3125

Montana

State Website	mt.gov
Health code and permits	dphs.mt.gov
Business Structure Filing	sos.mt.gov/Business/index.asp
Business Name Registration	sos.mt.gov/Business/index.asp
Business Tax Registration	app.mt.gov/bustax/
Information on Starting a Business	mt.gov/business.asp
Small Business Administration Office	sba.gov/about-offices-content/2/3126

Nebraska

State Website	nebraska.gov
Health code and permits	Contact your city or county health dept.
City or County Business Licenses	Contact your city or county health dept.
Business Structure Filing	sos.ne.gov/business/corp_serv/index.html
Business Name Registration	nebraska.gov/osbr/index.cgi

Business Tax Registration	revenue.state.ne.us/business/bus_regist.html
Information on Starting a Business	nebraska.gov/dynamicindex.html#
Small Business Administration Office	sba.gov/about-offices-content/2/3129

Nevada

State Website	nv.gov
Health code and permits	Contact your city or county health dept.
Food establishment rules:	leg.state.nv.us/NAC/NAC-446.html
Business Structure Filing	nvsos.gov/index.aspx?page=415
Business Name Registration	nvsos.gov/
Business Tax Registration	nevadatax.nv.gov/web/
Information on Starting a Business	diversifynevada.com/
Small Business Administration Office	sba.gov/about-offices-content/2/3133

New Hampshire

State Website	nh.gov
Home kitchen rules	dhhs.nh.gov/dphs/fp/sanitation/documents/hkbrochure.pdf
Business Structure Filing	sos.nh.gov/corporate/
Business Name Registration	sos.nh.gov/corporate/tradenameforms.html
Business Tax Registration	nh.gov/revenue/faq/gti-rev.htm
Starting a Business in NH	nheconomy.com/business-services/start-a-business-in-nh/
Small Business Administration Office	sba.gov/about-offices-content/2/3130

New Jersey

State Website	nj.gov
Health code and permits	Contact your city or county health dept.
City or County Business Licenses	Contact your city or county health dept.
Business Structure Filing	state.nj.us/treasury/revenue/dcr/filing/leadpg.htm
Business Name Registration	state.nj.us/njbgs/njbgsnar.htm
Business Tax Registration	state.nj.us/treasury/revenue/dcr/filing/leadpg.htm
Information on Starting a Business	nj.gov/njbusiness/
Small Business Administration Office	sba.gov/about-offices-content/2/3131

New Mexico

State Website	newmexico.gov
Health code and permits	Contact your city or county health dept.
City or County Business Licenses	Contact your city or county health dept.

Business Taxes	tax.newmexico.gov
Information on Starting a Business	newmexico.gov
Small Business Administration Office	sba.gov/localresources
Department of Agriculture.	nmdaweb.nmsu.edu/

New York

State Website	state.ny.us
Health code and permits	Contact your city or county health dept.
City or County Business Licenses	agmkt.state.ny.us/FS/license/pdfs/FSI-303.PDF
Business Structure Filing	nysegov.com/citGuide.cfm?superCat=28
Business Name Registration	dos.state.ny.us/corps/bus_entity_search.html
Business Tax Registration	tax.ny.gov/
Information on Starting a Business	nysegov.com/citGuide.cfm?superCat=28
Small Business Administration Office	sba.gov/about-offices-content/2/3135

North Carolina

State Website	ncgov.com
Health code and permits	ncalhd.org/county.htm
City or County Business Licenses	Contact your city or county health dept.
Business Structure Filing	secretary.state.nc.us/corporations/
Business Name Registration	thrivenc.com/smallbusiness/start-a-new-business
Business Tax Registration	dornc.com/forms/index.html
Information on Starting a Business	thrivenc.com/smallbusiness/start-a-new-business
Small Business Administration Office	sba.gov/about-offices-content/2/3127
Home Based Guidelines	agr.state.nc.us/fooddrug/food/homebiz.htm

North Dakota

State Website	nd.gov
Dept of Health, Division of Food and Lodging.	ndhealth.gov/foodlodging/
Business Structure Filing	nd.gov/sos/businessserv/
Business Name Registration	nd.gov/sos/businessserv/registrations/tradename.html
Business Tax Registration	nd.gov/businessreg/
Information on Starting a Business	nd.gov/category.htm?id=160
Small Business Administration Office	sba.gov/about-offices-content/2/3128

Ohio

State Website	ohio.gov
City or County Business Licenses	Contact your city or county health dept.
Ohio Dept. of Agriculture	foodsafety@agri.ohio.gov.
Business Structure Filing	sos.state.oh.us/businessServices.aspx
Business Name Registration	business.ohio.gov/starting/
Business Tax Registration	business.ohio.gov/efiling/
Information on Starting a Business	business.ohio.gov/
Small Business Administration Office	sba.gov/about-offices-content/2/3138
Licenses, Permits and Zoning	ohioline.osu.edu/cd-fact/1201.html

Oklahoma

State Website	ok.gov
Health code and permits	ok.gov/health/
City or County Business Licenses	Contact your city or county health dept.
Business Structure Filing	okcommerce.gov/sbrs/
Business Name Registration	sos.ok.gov/corp/filing.aspx
Business Tax Registration	tax.ok.gov/bustax.html
Information on Starting a Business	ok.gov/section.php?sec_id=4
Small Business Administration Office	sba.gov/about-offices-content/2/3139

Oregon

State Website	oregon.gov
Health code and permits	Contact your city or county health dept.
City or County Business Licenses	Contact your city or county health dept.
Business Structure Filing	filinginoregon.com/
Business Name Registration	secure.sos.state.or.us/ABNWeb/
Business Tax Registration	oregon.gov/DOR/BUS/index.shtml
Information on Starting a Business	oregon.gov/menu_files/business_kut.shtml
Small Business Administration Office	sba.gov/about-offices-content/2/3140
Domestic Kitchen website	oregon.gov/ODA/FSD/program_food.shtml

Pennsylvania

State Website	pa.gov
Health code and permits	http://www.agriculture.state.pa.us
City or County Business Licenses	Contact your city or county health dept.
Business Structure Filing	http://dos.state.pa.us
Business Name Registration	http://dos.state.pa.us
Business Tax Registration	http://www.revenue.state.pa.us
Information on Starting a Business	pa.gov/portal/server.pt/community/work/3015

| Small Business Administration Office | sba.gov/about-offices-content/2/3141 |

Rhode Island

State Website	ri.gov
Health code and permits	health.state.ri.us/licenses/food
City or County Business Licenses	Contact your city or county health dept.
Business Structure Filing	sos.ri.gov/business/filings/
Business Name Registration	Contact your city or town clerk
Business Tax Registration	ri.gov/taxation/BAR/
Information on Starting a Business	ri.gov/business/
Small Business Administration Office	sba.gov/about-offices-content/2/3144

South Carolina

State Website	sc.gov
Health code and permits	Contact your city or county health dept.
City or County Business Licenses	Contact your city or county health dept.
Department of Agriculture, Regulations	agriculture.sc.gov/foodsafetyandcompliance
Business Structure Filing	scsos.com/Business_Filings/
Business Name Registration	scsos.com/Business_Filings_FAQs
Business Tax Registration	scbos.sc.gov/
Information on Starting a Business	sc.gov/business/Pages/default.aspx
Small Business Administration Office	sba.gov/about-offices-content/2/31

South Dakota

State Website	sd.gov
Health code and permits	legis.state.sd.us/rules.
City or County Business Licenses	Contact your city or county health dept.
Guidelines:	doh.sd.gov/HealthProtection/guide.aspx
Business Structure Filing	sdsos.gov
Business Name Registration	https://apps.sd.gov/Applications
Business Tax Registration	apps.sd.gov/applications/rv23cedar/main/main.aspx
Information on Starting a Business	sd.gov/servicedirect/
Small Business Administration Office	sba.gov/about-offices-content/2/3146

Tennessee

State Website	tennessee.gov
Health code and permits	Contact your city or county health dept.
City or County Business Licenses	Contact your city or county health dept.
Business Structure Filing	tn.gov/sos/bus_svc/corpFAQs.htm
Business Name Registration	tnbear.tn.gov/Ecommerce/NameAvailability.aspx

Business Tax Registration	tn.gov/revenue/tntaxes/business.htm
Information on Starting a Business	tn.gov/topics/Business
Small Business Administration Office	sba.gov/about-offices-content/2/3147

Texas

State Website	texas.gov
Health code and permits	Contact your city or county health dept.
City or County Business Licenses	Contact your city or county health dept.
Dept of State Health Services, Food and Drug Licensing.	Department, 512 834 6626
Business Structure Filing	sos.state.tx.us/corp/index.shtml
Business Name Registration	sos.state.tx.us/
Business Tax Registration	window.state.tx.us/taxinfo/sales/new_business.html
Information on Starting a Business	www.texas.gov
Small Business Administration Office	sba.gov/about-offices-content/2/3148
Department of Agriculture.	texascottagefoodlaw.com/

Utah

State Website	utah.gov
Health code and permits	Contact your city or county health dept.
City or County Business Licenses	secure.utah.gov/osbr-user/user/welcome.html
Dept of Agriculture and Foods.	rules.utah.gov/publicat/code/r070/r070-560.htm
Business Structure Filing	utah.gov/business/starting/structure_starting.html
Business Name Registration	utah.gov/business/starting/structure_starting.html
Business Tax Registration	tax.utah.gov/business/information
Information on Starting a Business	business.utah.gov/
Small Business Administration Office	sba.gov/about-offices-content/2/3154

Vermont

State Website	vermont.gov
Health code and permits	healthvermont.gov/enviro/food_lodge/Bakeries.aspx
City or County Business Licenses	Contact your city or county health dept.
License application:	healthvermont.gov/
Business Structure Filing	sec.state.vt.us/corps/corpindex.htm
Business Name Registration	sec.state.vt.us/corps/forms/tradeapp.htm
Business Tax Registration	vermont.gov/portal/business/index.php?id=91

Information on Starting a Business   vermont.gov/portal/business/
Small Business Administration Office   sba.gov/about-offices-content/2/3156

Virginia

State Website	virginia.gov
Health code and permits	Contact your city or county health dept.
City or County Business Licenses	Contact your city or county health dept.
Business Structure Filing	scc.virginia.gov/clk/begin.aspx
Business Name Registration	scc.virginia.gov/clk/index.aspx
Business Tax Registration	tax.virginia.gov/site.cfm?alias=BusinessHome
Information on Starting a Business	portal.virginia.gov/business/
Small Business Administration Office	sba.gov/about-offices-content/2/3155

Washington

State Website	wa.gov
Health code and permits	Contact your city or county health dept.
City or County Business Licenses	bls.dor.wa.gov
Business Structure Filing	sos.wa.gov/corps/Default.aspx
Business Name Registration	bls.dor.wa.gov/
Business Tax Registration	dor.wa.gov/content/doingbusiness/registermybusiness/
Information on Starting a Business	access.wa.gov/business/start.aspx
Small Business Administration Office	sba.gov/about-offices-content/2/3157

West Virginia

State Website	wv.gov
Health code and permits	wvdhhr.org/phs/food/index.asp
City or County Business Licenses	Contact your city or county health dept.
Business Structure Filing	sos.wv.gov/Pages/default.aspx
Business Name Registration	sos.wv.gov/Pages/default.aspx
Business Tax Registration	wva.state.wv.us/wvtax/default.aspx
Information on Starting a Business	business4wv.com/b4wvpublic/default.aspx
Small Business Administration Office	sba.gov/about-offices-content/2/3159

Wisconsin

State Website	wisconsin.gov
Health code and permits	Contact your city or county health dept.
City or County Business Licenses	Contact your city or county health dept.
Food Business Innovation in Wisconsin	fyi.uwex.edu/foodbin/the-food-bin-network
Business Structure Filing	wdfi.org/corporations/forms/

Business Name Registration	wisconsin.gov/state/byb/name.html
Business Tax Registration	revenue.wi.gov/faqs/pcs/btr-on.html
Information on Starting a Business	wisconsin.gov/state/core/business.html
Small Business Administration Office	sba.gov/about-offices-content/2/3158

Wyoming

State Website	wyoming.gov
Health code and permits	Contact your city or county health dept.
City or County Business Licenses	Contact your city or county health dept.
Dept of Agriculture	wyagric.state.wy.us/divisions/chs/food-safety
Business Structure Filing	soswy.state.wy.us/Forms/FormsFiling.
aspx?startwith=Business	
Business Name Registration	soswy.state.wy.us/Forms/FormsFiling.
aspx?startwith=Business	
Business Tax Registration	revenue.state.wy.us
Info on Starting a Business	wyomingbusiness.org/program/starting-a-business/3413
Small Business Administration Office	sba.gov/about-offices-content/2/3160

The Brains Behind Your Cake Business!

Cake Whizz is a unique and easy to use piece of business software that will change your life!

Designed by a cake decorator with the input of hundreds of cake business professionals, *Cake Whizz* was created specifically to simplify and organize the way you run your cake business!

Simply input your recipes, and the cost of all your ingredients and cake making supplies and *'CLICK'* to view and use your very own *Cake Whizz*:

★ **Pricing Calculator:** Calculate the exact cost of every cake, and the profit for every order. Never undercharge again!

★ **Dashboard:** Displays upcoming orders, overdue and due payments, and monthly totals to date. Track all your business expenses, and create reports to show you exactly where your money is coming from and going to.

★ **Orders:** View all the information relevant to each order. Attach photos, sketches and customer comments to each order so it's all in one place.

★ **Invoices:** Create custom invoices with your own logo and info. Add tax, discounts, and set payment deadline reminders.

★ **Calendar:** Orders are automatically added to the planning calendar. Add your own appointments too, and view by day, week, month or year.

★ **Customer Database:** View customer contact information, birthdays and anniversaries, and order history. Create anniversary alerts—perfect for follow-up business opportunities.

★ **Shopping Lists:** *Cake Whizz* calculates exactly what you need for upcoming orders—just click and print. Never run out of ingredients or supplies again!

★ **Recipe Screen:** Enter your most used recipes and easily cost out every single ingredient you use. Price of an ingredient changed? Just update once and 'CLICK'—*Cake Whizz* will instantly update the costings for ALL of your recipes and pending orders AND Cake Whizz easily coverts recipes and ingredients to/from grams/ounces/ml etc.

★ **Use *Cake Whizz* Anywhere:** Log into your account from any computer you like—whether it's the PC in the dining room, laptop on the sofa, i-pad in the kitchen or i-phone at a wedding fair! Stored on a secure server, only *YOU* can view your own customer and order information!

Cake Whizz takes the headache out of cake business admin, leaving you free to do what you do best—create beautiful cakes!

For tons more info, screen shots, FAQ's and Tutorials visit:

www.cakewhizz.com

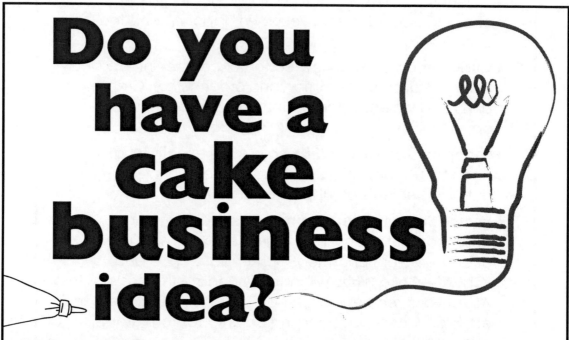

CPSIA information can be obtained at www.ICGtesting.com
Printed in the USA
LVOW031701200512

282475LV00002BA/1/P